Off the Grid

Off the Grid
Houses for Escape
-

Dominic Bradbury

310 illustrations

Contents

Introduction

One of the greatest delights of off-grid living is the special sense of freedom it offers. Rooted in a true appreciation of the beauty of the natural world, the concept of a twenty-first-century self-sufficient home creates a golden opportunity to liberate oneself from traditional networks, whether physical or social, and make a free choice about how and where to live. Breaking the conventional reliance on standard utility services and infrastructure requires a degree of imagination and confidence, but also allows a wealth of possibilities that make everyday living in remote and rural parts of the world a rewarding and tempting reality.

Advances in home-generated renewable energy have made the process of going off-grid more practical and affordable than ever, allowing opportunities for escapism and total immersion in natural surroundings far away from the constant pressures of everyday living in cities and towns. As well as providing the context for a more meaningful sense of connection with nature, off-grid living is deeply in tune with the green imperative to reduce our environmental footprint and our damaging reliance on fossil fuels.

In a thoughtful and considered way, self-sufficient homes address heartfelt contemporary concerns about both conservation and connectivity. Modern self-sufficiency is rooted in respect for the landscape and a true understanding of local and natural resources. But the twenty-first-century off-grid home also builds on fresh architectural understanding, new engineering and rapid advances in materials such as glazing and insulation, as well as micropower-generation technology.

The green imperative

We must reduce our carbon footprint and refocus on renewable sources of energy, and this reality is clearly having a profound impact at all levels of society. Off-grid living brings these concerns down to a personal level, presenting a series of options for how we design, heat and power our homes. Some of these options are deeply familiar and reassuringly low-tech, such as wood-burning stoves, private wells and rainwater harvesting. Yet many others have only opened up – or have at least become more efficient and accessible – over recent decades, including photovoltaics, domestic battery storage, heat pumps of various kinds and small-scale wind and hydroelectric turbines.

Combining such systems and technology in ways that are suited to the particular context and conditions of a site makes off-grid living viable in a range of circumstances. In this respect, advances in the microgeneration of power and heat have created opportunities for everyday living in more isolated environments, from islands to mountainsides to deserts and other remote countryside locations. Yet the question of home energy really must be seen as part of a more complex design-and-build equation that assumes special importance in areas of environmental sensitivity.

Planning controls restrict or prevent building in areas of special scientific interest and protected habitats, such as national parks and wildlife reserves. Yet any kind of construction should carry with it a degree of responsibility, which will always be felt more acutely in remote and fragile parts of the countryside or coast. In that respect, as can be seen throughout the projects in this book, limiting the size, height and scale of the building itself will not only help to reduce its visual impact in the landscape, but also cut down

its energy and water needs. Consciously reducing the requirements and overall footprint of a house, with all the spaces and functions it contains, is a key part of a more sustainable approach to design.

Beyond that, the notion of treading as lightly as possible upon the land – promoted and encouraged over many decades by pioneers such as the Australian architect Glenn Murcutt – has become more embedded than ever, especially in relation to rural residences. It applies to the way in which a house is positioned and built, with a growing popularity in the use of pillars and piloti to provide platforms for living that are raised above the earth while causing minimal damage to it. Increasingly, there is a sense that such buildings in sensitive locations should be regarded as temporary rather than permanent, capable of being removed and recycled relatively easily, leaving little or no trace on the land.

This philosophy extends to the landscaping around such buildings, which is generally kept to a minimum in a respectful process of immersion rather than adaptation. In some instances, where the environment has already been damaged in some way – perhaps by intensive farming, grazing, fire or earlier settlement – off-grid owners have embarked on careful programmes of land restoration and conservation, using only indigenous planting that should benefit local wildlife. Such decisions are informed by an awareness of the fact that water is also a precious natural resource, and one that may not be readily available in more extreme climates.

The idea of a light touch also extends to the choice of materials. Clearly, the overall carbon footprint of a home is dictated not just by the amount – or type – of energy it consumes each day,

Each house that we explore in this book provides its residents with a retreat of one kind or another, in some of the world's most extraordinary and beautiful natural settings

but also by the resources that are consumed during the construction process. Most new natural homes adopt an organic palette, and – since timber from sustainable forestry is one of the greenest possible materials, sucking in carbon and breathing out oxygen as it grows – many of the houses in this book are modern variants on the wooden cabin. Recycled materials, too, are common in the houses in these pages.

Passive design plays a vital part in the design and build of off-grid houses and organic homes. Architects begin the design process by studying and responding to the position and climatic conditions of a site. Solar gain – the process of drawing on the natural heat of the sun – is maximized during the colder months and mitigated (by overhanging eaves, shutters or verandas, for example) in high summer. Natural ventilation techniques are also part of thoughtful passive design, embracing cross-ventilation and also heat stacks that draw hot air up through a building and exhaust it from the top, eliminating the need for energy-hungry air-conditioning systems.

A common-sense passive design approach carries through to the envelope of the building, using layers of high-performance insulation to help regulate the internal temperature of the house. The same is true of contemporary glazing, which has changed in recent years from double-glazed to triple-glazed systems, radically reducing a major source of energy loss. Heat-recovery systems can also reduce the amount of energy that flows needlessly out of the home.

Such strategies cut down on the energy a house requires and consumes. This, in turn, reduces the amount of heat and power that must be generated in the first instance, making the goal of self-sufficiency more attainable. It is a holistic approach, in which the ultimate choice of energy generation will be largely dictated by the conditions of the site. Solar, wind or other systems, often in conjunction with low-tech solutions such as wood-burners, can help to create fully independent escapist homes that do not rely on standard utilities.

Rural retreats

Breaking those connections to the grid is a liberating process in itself, with all the implicit satisfaction of independence and self-reliance. Such homes can truly be described as retreats, places where it is possible to step back from grids and screens in order to recharge and reconnect with nature rather than networks. This theme of retreat surfaces again and again in the projects that follow, with individuals and families anxious to step back and reassess their lives and lifestyles.

Off-grid living can be linked to the growing trend for digital detoxification, where we power down for a few hours or days at a time in the hope of reducing our reliance on twenty-four-hour news and feedback loops. For families, in particular, with children exposed to constant digital temptation and peer pressure, the notion of a true retreat may be particularly appealing. But the same might be said for artists, writers and creative thinkers of all kinds seeking mental and physical space, while perhaps also drawing inspiration from nature itself. As such, we are still following the example of Henry David Thoreau and looking for our own Walden Pond. Many would say that the need for our own beloved Walden is more desperate than ever.

The owner of the Gordon Ozarks Cabin (see page 28) in the forests of Arkansas talks of a place 'to meditate, to write and to get away from the stresses of everyday life'. The architect Jesse Garlick describes his own self-designed hilltop home (see page 124) as 'a place to contemplate the world'. Robert Brown, the architect of Permanent Camping in the Australian outback (see page 24), talks of the way that the building 'represents many people's dream of a simple life – a getaway from reality and a place to be with nature'. Similar sentiments prevail in other corners of the world.

Another of the great advantages of digital detox is a resetting of the body clock to natural rhythms that are more in tune with diurnal and seasonal change. As well as connecting with the landscape, stepping away from the swamp of artificial urban light allows a fuller appreciation of the night sky and the stars, and engagement with sunset and dawn. Such thinking helped to inspire projects such as Waind Gohil + Potter Architects' SkyHut in Wales (see page 166), with its retractable observatory-style roof, and David and Susan Scott's Alpine Cabin on Vancouver Island (see page 130), where the lighting comes from candles and the 'extraordinary display of stars in the night sky' is one of the delights of being in the house. At Camp Baird in California (see page 92), the carefully considered design of the cabin encourages the family to 'spend nearly every waking hour outdoors', while the bedrooms are little more than night-time bunkrooms.

Each house that we explore in this book provides its residents with a retreat of one kind or another, in some of the world's most extraordinary and beautiful natural settings. Some are extreme and challenging places, in terms not only of the changing seasons, but also of accessibility. But that is part of the adventure, of course: whether arriving by boat, on foot or even on horseback, the journey itself is part of the exhilarating pleasure of escapism.

Most of the houses in these pages are fully off-grid in terms of energy, water and other resources. Some could be described as 'net zero' rather than fully off-grid, meaning that a cable connection to the electrical grid allows an excess of self-generated, renewable energy to be sold for use elsewhere, along with the option to draw back at times of peak demand. In the future, fresh advances in home battery storage will make such an arrangement less of a temptation. A few are largely self-sufficient, but draw on local sources of green energy in places like Tasmania or Norway, where hydroelectric power is dominant. In such cases, where renewable energy is readily available, the temptation to explore a connection becomes strong – as long as it is practical – even for those with the very greenest intentions. Finally, there are occasional instances where the journey to full self-sufficiency is a work in progress, and the last parts of the green jigsaw are still waiting to be slotted into place.

All these homes, however, are solid examples of a wide range of off-grid systems and energy strategies, along with passive design ideas that help to conserve heat and power. Such eco-cabins and rural retreats suggest how a creative and contextual combination of architectural, technical and philosophical thinking enables a way of life that is both liberating and responsible.

Countryside
and Forest

The ambition of living lightly upon the land takes on many different aspects when it comes to house and home. The overarching ideal of making the smallest possible impact on the landscapes we love leads to an approach that inevitably combines complementary decisions about lifestyle, renewable energy, landscaping and, of course, the architectural design and construction of the home itself. It is a holistic outlook, at best, which places respect for the landscape and the natural environment at its heart.

Within the sensitive surroundings of the countryside and forest, respect for the notion of living lightly upon the land assumes particular importance given the delicacy of complex ecosystems and the intricate threads that hold them together. In this context, the conservation, generation and consumption of energy are one part of a complex series of decisions that collectively make the difference between a new natural house that respects the rural location in which it sits and one that simply intends to impose itself on the landscape, regardless of context. Passive design strategies, such as high levels of insulation, double or triple glazing and consideration of solar gain, reduce energy consumption in a sensitively conceived building, while renewable and home-grown sources of energy such as solar and wind power help to create an independent and self-sufficient home without drawing from the grid or relying on fossil fuels. Rainwater harvesting or private wells help to manage and preserve another key resource, and in such ways the environmental footprint of the home is significantly reduced.

Yet in rural settings in particular, sensitivity to the land also involves other vital considerations that contribute to the goal of touching the earth as lightly and carefully as possible. In the countryside such ambitions can be met only with a true understanding of the unique character and conditions of the setting, and a contextual architectural approach that forms a direct and considered response to nature in its widest sense, including topography, the movement of the sun and the impact of wind and weather.

The story of each contextual home begins with a careful process of research, in the hope of gaining a deeper knowledge of the specific subtleties of the site and setting. In this sense, the houses in these pages are 'organic' (as Frank Lloyd Wright and others used the word): the buildings themselves have evolved in a direct response to the landscape, and views and vistas have been carefully considered, as has the way the house sits discreetly and naturally within the contours of the land.

In this respect, the model of farmsteads and barns is a strong point of reference, as much as the powerful architectural and environmental lessons of such 'green' modernist architects as Wright, Geoffrey Bawa and Glenn Murcutt. Traditionally, farm buildings have evolved in a close and symbiotic relationship with the countryside, and farmhouses, barns and other structures sit in naturally sheltered positions in a formation that partially encloses courtyards or other outdoor spaces. Construction materials are gathered nearby, adding to the strongly localized quality of the farmstead. This model of contextuality continues to be vital in the design of homes that work with rather than against their surroundings.

Midland Architecture's Off-Grid Retreat on a family farm in Belmont County, Ohio (see page 38), draws inspiration from vernacular farm buildings, although the architectural solutions are distinctly modern. The same is true of Studio Moffitt's House on Limekiln Line in Huron County, Ontario (see page 46). Here, a modestly scaled new home sits easily in the arable farmland, forming a vivid and direct relationship with the open fields of wheat and barley. The physical impact of the house upon the landscape is small, and so is its overall carbon footprint.

There is an essential modesty of scale in such houses, and the model of the cabin forms another important point of reference for green living. Rather like farmhouses and barns, the cabin is a building born of the landscape, and it represents another contextual typology in terms of site and position, as well as the use of materials. By their very nature, cabins are modest in scale and intention, often created for summer or holiday use and executed with a degree of subtlety.

The romantic ideal of the cabin implies escapism and tranquility, tied to remote and beautiful natural settings that deserve green, organic and low-impact architecture. DEN Architecture's Gordon Ozarks Cabin in Arkansas was designed as a modern and fully self-sufficient retreat in the woods (see page 28) and as a place to think, recharge and meditate. Misho + Associates Premaydena House on the Tasman Peninsula, Tasmania (see page 42), was designed and built with a similar philosophy: to create a modest, contextual escape closely tied to a mesmerizing rural setting, requiring little maintenance and with the smallest possible environmental footprint.

Such rural retreats form not only escapes from the pressure of the everyday world, but also enriching sources of inspiration, as seen in FLOAT Architectural Research and Design's Watershed cabin in Oregon (see page 52), a creative hub for a nature writer and philosopher. This self-sufficient, off-grid building lays the lightest of touches, or caresses, on the land and can be removed (or 'demounted') at the end of its useful life with minimal impact.

Watershed's intriguing hybrid of cabin and camping hut is seen in a number of other off-grid structures, such as Casey Brown Architecture's Permanent Camping in New South Wales, Australia (see page 24), which is accessible only on horseback or foot and is used for weekend adventures. Similarly, JeanArch's 72H Cabin in Dalsland, Sweden (see page 78), is intended as a short-term escape requiring only the most basic provisions and services. Such hybrids offer a way of communing directly and positively with the surroundings while having little impact on the land. They offer a fresh model of living, in which the needs and requirements of everyday life are reduced to a minimum, allowing a purer focus on the natural wonders of the surroundings.

Floating in Farmland Meadows

—

arba-: Maison Barache, Auvilliers, Normandy, France

Left The timber framework is expressed internally in spaces such as this attic bedroom, which has a simple cabin aesthetic.

Opposite Cedar shingles clad the exterior walls and the roof, lending the cabin sculptural purity and simplicity.

Countryside and Forest

Below A large wood-burning stove provides heat for the house; the brick surround and chimney store warmth and distribute it through the building.

Right and opposite The simple kitchen, also made from plywood and timber, flows out on to a deck, an outdoor dining space that looks across the meadow.

The architect Jean-Baptiste Barache describes his off-grid country home as an experiment rather than a statement. Sometimes called 'the house in a field', Maison Barache is a low-tech solution to the challenge of self-building a rural escape with simple materials and a modest budget. The result is a timber-framed home, coated in shingles, which echoes the barns and agricultural buildings of the region. The pinewood frame, which appears to float upon concrete piers embedded in the field, is the only element that wasn't built by Barache himself, who completed the project over a period of two years.

Barache, whose architectural practice, arba-, is based in Paris, found a bucolic and tempting site in open pasture bordered by woodland near a small commune between Rouen and Amiens. The exterior, including the sharply pitched roof, is clad in a skin of red cedar shingles, lending the house an organic quality. At one end, a large wall of glass has been inserted into the A-frame, allowing natural sunlight to flood in and dissolve the boundary between the main living space and the wooden deck alongside, complete with outdoor dining table and seating. This glass façade is pierced by louvres, which help to cool the house during the summer.

The interior is arranged over three levels. The ground floor is partially open-plan, with fluid connections between the main living room to the front and the kitchen/dining area behind; a triple-height space facing the deck gives a striking impression of height and scale. The staircase and the single bathroom are in the centre. Three simple, cabin-style bedrooms are at mid-level, and the master bedroom is held on a slim upper storey within the tip of the pitchedroof. The joinery and partitioning throughout are of simple veneered timber, plywood and chipboard.

The main source of heat in this off-grid home is a wood-burning stove, which distributes warmth throughout via a brick surround and chimney. The simple kitchen stove is powered by a gas canister, and the water is from a private source. Without any electricity, Barache and his Japanese wife, Mie, rely on oil lamps, although they are considering installing solar panels and battery storage. 'I love the light of a flame and the way it creates shadows,' says Barache. 'It's a very Japanese notion – beauty that does not reveal itself.'

The house also respects its rural setting, and little or no landscaping has been done around it. During the summer, Maison Barache appears to float in the green meadow, a natural presence in the landscape.

An Escape Among the Trees

-

BarlisWedlick Architects: Fox Hall,
Ancram, New York, USA

Opposite and page 21 The tower holding the sauna, a screened dining area and a lookout post is connected to the body of the house by an elevated walkway.

Above The main seating area looks out into the woods through a floor-to-ceiling window that connects the house to the landscape.

When Ian Hague started thinking about building a rural retreat for himself and his family, the ambition of net zero living was a priority. As a fund manager in New York, Hague has worked in parts of the world where sustainability has not always been of great concern. For his own home he wanted to follow his own preoccupations and create something that would truly be 'light on the land'.

Settling on a 30-hectare (75-acre) estate in Columbia County, with views of the Catskills and the Berkshires from the highest point, Hague began working with the architectural practice BarlisWedlick on a phased approach to create a private compound of complementary buildings. They began with a barn, built with a restored frame dating from the 1840s, complete with a self-contained apartment. The barn house, which provided Hague with a place to stay on the estate while other works progressed, was fitted with a substantial solar array on its roof and battery storage in the basement.

'One of the directives when we first met Ian was that the property should be self-sustaining,' says the architect Alan Barlis. 'We look at the whole estate as a place where Ian makes more power than he uses, and so we are net zero. The capacity of the solar array on the barn is much bigger than you would ever need for the barn

itself, so he can charge his electric car from the batteries or use the energy elsewhere so that he can be off-grid.'

Having finished the barn, complete with natural swimming pool alongside, BarlisWedlick designed a house further up the hill, to serve as a more private retreat for Ian and his grown-up children. This building is relatively modest in scale, with a master suite, open-plan living spaces and a guest bedroom and den. Other parts of the programme were included in a separate tower nearby. This holds a sauna heated by a wood-burning stove at ground level, an open-air dining room above and, at the top, a lookout post among the treetops.

The property has its own water sources and septic field, and Hague plans to increase the provision of renewable energy over time. He also means to build a guest house. It was important to him to build with materials – especially timber – that were either reclaimed or from sustainable sources.

The property serves as a very personal escape, but one that also offers an exemplar for green living in the midst of nature. 'I love the fact that it's so different here in every season,' says Hague. 'You get these wonderful but different impressions of the land and the trees that change over the months. You begin to feel it as you come up the driveway, and all your cares melt away.'

Page 20 and above The master bedroom sits on a mezzanine, overlooking the open-plan dining and seating area, with the kitchen to one side.

Left This open-air dining room, protected by fly-screen mesh walls, sits at mid-level in the tower built alongside the house.

Opposite The main living areas are in a double-height space at one end of the house, where the timber structure is clearly visible.

Returning to Simplicity in the Outback

—

Casey Brown Architecture: Permanent Camping,
Mudgee, New South Wales, Australia

The micro-cabin has a sleeping loft on the upper level, accessed via a ladder and hatch.

The name Mudgee, which is derived from a Wiradjuri Aboriginal word, means 'nest in the hills'. It's a beautifully apposite term for this building by Casey Brown Architecture, perched on a hillside. Something between a residence and a temporary outback camp, Permanent Camping is a fully self-sufficient retreat in an area that has no mains services. Like a camping pavilion or simple cabin, it has the feel of a temporary structure erected in the landscape.

The town of Mudgee, about 275 kilometres (170 miles) northwest of Sydney, grew quickly during the gold rush of the 1850s, and later became known for agriculture, wool and wine. Casey Brown's client grew up on a sheep farm nearby, and has fond memories of camping on the land as a child, going to and from the site on horseback.

The request was for a weekend retreat suited to this remote location, which has neither road access nor neighbours. 'We wanted something comfortable, warm and architectural, that could be left unattended and still be safe and secure from the elements,' says the owner of Permanent Camping. 'We also wanted the building to sit comfortably in the landscape. We love the simplicity and serenity it provides, while being an original work of art.'

Casey Brown developed a lightweight design that was largely prefabricated in Sydney, with a recycled ironbark timber frame and corrugated copper cladding. Copper shutters on the ground floor of the two-storey structure form canopies when raised, creating a series of verandas, and protect the building and its glass windows when lowered. Inside the ground floor is a simple, multifunctional space arranged around a wood-burning stove, with an integrated sink and storage unit on one wall. A ladder ascends to a sleeping loft with floors, window frames and other joinery in ironbark.

Permanent Camping has no access to electricity or other services. Rainwater is collected on the roof and stored in a tank at the back of the house; a wood-burning stove and oil lamps provide heat and light in the winter, and in the summer the building is ventilated naturally. Toilet facilities are in a separate micro structure nearby. The entire building was designed to be as low-maintenance as possible.

'It is one step up from camping,' says the architect Robert Brown. 'It's warm in freezing conditions and gives protection from fire, wind, snow and rain. It's a minimal shelter for living in nature with a minimal footprint and a rustic or rugged exterior but fine interior joinery. We like the way the building represents many people's dream of a simple life – a getaway from reality and a place to be with nature, yet still comfortable and safe.'

Opposite There is no road access to Permanent Camping, so the only way to reach it is by riding or hiking.

Left and below The lower level contains a wood-burning stove, a sink mounted against one wall and simple seating.

A Meditative Woodland Retreat

-

DEN Architecture: Gordon Ozarks Cabin,
Ozark Mountains, Arkansas, USA

The house platform floats over the ground, with the aim of minimizing the structure's impact on the natural environment.

'It is meant to be a home for retreat ... I use the house to meditate, to write and to get away from the stresses of everyday life.'

Above and right Living spaces are soothing and simple, with high ceilings, timber floors and close connections to the outside.

Opposite The house has an integrated veranda, which takes the form of an observation deck looking out into the woods.

Overleaf The meditation room, at the heart of the calm, offers a framed view of the trees.

Situated in a remote Arkansas enclave, the Gordon Ozarks Cabin is a true retreat in every sense of the word. Commissioned by an entrepreneur and doctor of Chinese medicine, Jason Gordon, the house sits on the large estate of a Buddhist community in the Ozark Mountains. The land is accessible only by off-road vehicles and has no standard utility services; each home sits in a 2-hectare (5-acre) parcel.

Gordon's cabin floats in a gently sloping wooded landscape, raised above the ground on pillars. 'It is meant to be a home for retreat and meditation,' he says. 'The environmental consciousness of the home and its independence are important to that intention. I use the house to meditate, to write and to get away from the stresses of everyday life.'

Gordon turned to the architect Germán Brun of Miami-based practice DEN Architecture, whom he first met through membership of a local soccer team. The commission for the Gordon Osarks Cabin represented both a challenge, in terms of building a home in this remote setting with minimal disturbance to the environment, and an opportunity to create a rounded, thoughtful and modern off-grid residence.

'The natural surroundings define everything in this setting, including the architecture,' says Brun. 'It's one of the most pristine and inaccessible locations in continental America. A strong sense of connection to the surrounding environment was a given, and we wanted the project to be as sustainable as possible without the stigma or look of a granola hippie bungalow.'

Sitting on its floating platform, the house was constructed to maximize solar gain in the winter and to make the most of natural ventilation in the summer. The heavily insulated envelope is a framework of local pine, clad for the most part in low-maintenance cement-board siding. There are two bedrooms, a meditation room and a generous, open-plan living area with a wood-burning stove to one side, with a slate surround; various integrated verandas and decks help to dissolve the distinction between indoor and outdoor space.

Creating a fully self-sufficient home required a range of technology, drawing on renewable sources and taking up one fifth of the modest cost of the house. A loop system providing hot water and radiant underfloor heating is fed by a combination of a biomass boiler, the stove in the living room and a heat exchanger that retains and redistributes warmth. Water comes from two large storage tanks fed by rainwater, while a solar array with battery storage provides electricity. Propane gas tanks can be used as a back-up if required. Isolated in the most inviting way possible, the house can operate entirely off-grid. More than that, it is an exemplar of a contemporary cabin that makes little or no demand on the landscape it inhabits.

An Organic Farmstead for the 21st Century

-

Henning Larsen Architects:
Granja Experimental Alnardo,
Valladolid, Castilla y León, Spain

Tucked into its sloping site, the farmhouse offers semi-private guest accommodation on the lower floor, private family space at the top and more social areas in between.

The winemaker Peter Sisseck has long been committed to biodynamic methods of production. This holistic organic philosophy has governed his work in Ribera del Duero, Spain, where he produces the celebrated Dominio de Pingus from his own vineyards. As part of an all-encompassing approach, Sisseck decided to create his own sustainable farmstead, which would allow him full control over the formulation of the organic compost that nourishes his vines, as well as providing him with a new home.

Having worked with Henning Larsen Architects on a bodega for his other label, PSI, the Danish-born Sisseck asked the practice to design a farmstead on 20 hectares (50 acres) of land in Castilla y León, northwestern Spain. Given the remote setting, well away from mains services, the farmstead was designed to be self-sufficient and off-grid. 'It's been an ambition to create a farm for quite some time, and now that it's up and running it's proving to be one of the best decisions we ever made,' says Sisseck. 'We are using the old methods of wine production and it's really important for the vineyards that we stimulate them in an organic way, because you need a lot of micro-organisms in the soil. Here we can guarantee that the compost is 100 per cent organic, which is important for the quality control of our vineyards.'

The farm revolves around a modest herd of dairy cows, which feed on its pastures; in the future Sisseck also hopes to produce an artisanal cheese using the milk they produce. The farm buildings include a milking parlour and storage spaces, while a little further up the mill Henning Larsen designed a twenty-first-century farmhouse that combines private escapes for Sisseck and his partner, more 'public' spaces for entertaining visitors, and semi-private accommodation for guests. The design of the house, led by the architect Ingela Larsson, allows great flexibility of use, and parts of the building – which is arranged around a central courtyard – open or close according to need. A separate pool and pool house are nearby, while landscape design by Tom Stuart-Smith makes the most of indigenous plants and shrubs.

The farm has its own water source, as well as the facilities to harvest and store rainwater, and a solar array near the farm buildings provides electricity. The chief source of heat is a biomass boiler, which is currently fed by wood pellets but could be fuelled by cuttings from the vineyards in the future. There is also an independent back-up generator for use in the winter, if required.

'From a purely practical point of view, it was important to be self-sufficient,' says Sisseck, 'because the infrastructure here is non-existent. We could have brought in an electrical line, but the connection is so far away that it would have cost a lot of money. We also tried to use local materials, and built the house with local artisans. It is a personal project, but also a wonderful collaboration with people who have a real talent for architecture and landscape design.'

Opposite Important living spaces such as the sitting room/library flow onto elevated balconies, to connect with the capitvating views of the countryside beyond.

This page As well as connecting with the open landscape, the house revolves around a hidden courtyard with a pool that helps to cool the building in the summer. The kitchen is also a pivotal space, connecting with the internal courtyard to one side and a small terrace to the other.

Waking to a View of the Lake

—

Midland Architecture: Off-Grid Retreat,
Belmont County, Ohio, USA

Opposite Set on a rise overlooking a freshwater lake, the cabin is high enough to offer a tempting vantage point.

Below The house sits on the borderland between forest and clearing, and the verdant woodland forms a vivid natural backdrop.

Countryside and Forest

There is a powerful aspect of liberation in the decision to go off-grid. Instead of worrying about how best to access existing services and utilities, there is the freedom to position a building in direct response to the landscape. Rather than compromising with a location that is better suited to bringing in power lines or water pipes, the selection of the right spot is guided by imagination and ambition.

This was certainly the case when Greg Dutton of Midland Architecture designed an off-grid retreat for his parents, John and Rita. The family own a cattle ranch in Belmont County, Ohio, which is home to 500 head of black Angus. The 405-hectare (1,000-acre) farm was once part of a surface coal-mining operation, but the land has been reclaimed and replanted as a mixture of pasture and woodland. Dutton's father had long dreamed of building an escapist cabin on the farm, and so Greg drew up the plans as a Father's Day gift and began building the cabin the following autumn.

'The programme was pretty simple,' says Dutton. 'The intention was to create a place for family gatherings, and my parents wanted a view of the surrounding landscape. So there's a large family room, or gathering space, and a couple of bedrooms. The choice to build the cabin with as little reliance on public utilities as possible allowed us flexibility over where we sited it, so we chose a spot overlooking the lake. You wake up in the morning and watch the sun rise through the hills and over the spine of the lake.'

The design of the cabin is inspired by the vernacular farm buildings and barns of the region. Set on a small rise and backed by woodland, the single-storey house has a timber frame, charred cedar cladding and a roof of Corten steel. The two bedrooms are at one end, and the open-plan family room and kitchen at the other open on to a covered porch, complete with an open-air dining table and an outdoor wood-burning fireplace for the colder months.

Water comes from a natural spring close by, filtered by sand and clay before use. Electricity is provided by an array of photovoltaic panels near the cabin, which also uses solar gain to warm the heavily insulated spaces; natural ventilation is used in the heat of summer. A back-up generator powered by propane gas tanks is available in case of additional energy needs.

There is a combined garage and store nearby, while an open-sided pavilion stands on the shore of the lake, forming a partially sheltered space for events with family and friends. In this way, the cabin is part of a cluster of small structures that resemble a farmstead in themselves.

Opposite An open-sided timber-framed pavilion on the shore is a partially sheltered space for family gatherings and events.

Left The living spaces have open views of the lake.

Below and bottom A veranda at one end of the cabin has a wood-burning fireplace, meaning that this open-air room can still be used in the colder months.

41

Cocooned from the Elements

-

Misho + Associates: Premaydena House,
Premaydena, Tasman Peninsula,
Tasmania, Australia

Layers of sliding doors and shutters allow the house to be closed securely when not in use, while also providing access to a wraparound veranda.

43

The Premaydena House, in the southeastern corner of Tasmania, encapsulates the green preoccupations of both architect and client in a thoughtful and succinct manner. They had worked together once before, when David Burns and his partner Tania Soghomonian commissioned the architect Misho Vasiljevich to work on their house in Sydney, where they still spend much of the year. Vasiljevich then made the move to Tasmania, building an off-grid home for himself, which helped to inspire the evolution of the Premaydena House.

Burns and Soghomonian, who work in the field of environmental sustainability, acquired a 19-hectare (47-acre) parcel of land on the Tasman Peninsula with the aim of building an off-grid retreat of their own. The house is in an elevated position on a hillside, backed by eucalyptus woodland, and looks out across the rural landscape and towards the waters of Norfolk Bay. Since it is used for periods of four or five weeks at a time, it was important that it be not only self-sufficient but also low-maintenance, and that it could be closed down and secured when not in use.

'The clients wanted an escape, something similar to where I live myself,' says Vasiljevich. 'They asked for two bedrooms and they wanted to be able to walk away and lock it up. So we designed a house that is compact and human and has a low impact on the environment, using a modular grid and components that maximize material usage and minimize material wastage.'

The house is essentially a box within a box. A steel frame combined with sliding metal screens forms a protective outer shell;

the ochre colour of these panels recalls a vivid lichen found on the local beaches. The screens open to reveal the house within, made with a frame of local timber and a combination of sliding timber panels and double-glazed windows, which also retract. Between these two flexible layers, which recall Japanese shoji screens, sits a timber deck that forms a borderland all the way around the building, and a zone that is sheltered from wind and sun.

Inside, an open-plan living space at one end of the house is warmed by a wood-burning stove, while two compact bedrooms are at the other end. At the centre is a service core with two en-suite shower rooms and a small laundry/utility room. Additional light is fed into the interior through a clerestory window on the zinc-coated roof, where a ramp protects the windows and offers the perfect base for a 5-kilowatt photovoltaic solar array plus solar tubes for generating hot water. There are water storage tanks and a waste-water treatment system that provides irrigation for new and indigenous planting around the house. Materials were obtained locally as far as possible.

'Misho selected a site for us that was nestled into the landscape and protected, forming a suntrap in the winter, but that also gives us the big views,' says Burns. 'It was extremely important to us to be self-sufficient and not to rely on any external systems. It's somewhere that we can really recharge and soak in the environment, where we can enjoy the openness on a warm, sunny day but also create a cocoon when it's wild outside.'

Opposite and right The main living spaces are open-plan, heated by a wood-burning stove.

Below The eucalyptus woods provide shelter and security, ensuring that the house never feels too exposed.

An Outpost in the Huron Pastures

—

Studio Moffitt: House on Limekiln Line,
Huron County, Ontario, Canada

Opposite The house sits among 10 hectares (25 acres) in an area devoted to arable farming, with sweeping views of fields, pasture and woodland.

Left and above A long raised walkway extends from the house into the pasture, forming a kind of lookout station in the landscape.

47

'The house acts as a place
of observation of the beautiful,
shifting landscape beyond, and
a place of cathartic respite.'

Above and right The interiors are light and
fluid, with contrasts in height and volume.

Opposite The house's open setting gives
the impression of a sculpted form floating
in the countryside.

Designing an off-grid home is about much more than making the most of self-generated energy. Thoughtful projects begin with an understanding of how best to reduce the energy needs of a building from the very start, while making the most of passive strategies such as solar gain and natural ventilation. These considerations were fundamental to Studio Moffitt's approach to the design of the House on Limekiln Line, which began with an extremely detailed study of the landscape and the natural conditions of the site.

The setting is certainly sublime. The client, Maggie Treanor, acquired a 10-hectare (25-acre) site in rural Huron County, in an area largely devoted to arable farming; much of her own land is leased back to local farmers, who grow wheat and barley in the fields that surround the house. Treanor turned to the architect Lisa Moffitt, who happens to be her son's partner, to commission a house that would be off-grid and that would make the most of the wide views of the countryside.

'It was very important to me that the house be off-grid,' says Treanor, who lives in it full-time. 'I felt it was time we all started to be more conscious of how large our footprint is on this beautiful planet. My son told me that Lisa would design a little jewel box for me to live in, and she certainly did.'

Moffitt's careful studies of the site led her to a design that is modest in scale but large in ambition. Limiting the house to about 92 square metres (just under 1,000 square feet) has reduced its overall energy consumption, especially in conjunction with triple glazing and a heavily insulated envelope. Substantial glazing frames important sight lines, and introduces a rich quality of sunlight that reduces the need for artificial lighting. The design also maximizes solar gain in the winter and reduces overheating in the summer, when the house is ventilated naturally.

The outline of the house is inspired by local farm buildings, and features a substantial porch and an elevated observation walkway that extends into the pasture alongside. Materials were obtained locally or regionally, and local artisans and farmers built the house. 'I wanted the design to limit the building and resource footprint without compromising the expansiveness of the landscape,' says Moffitt. 'The house acts as a place of observation of the beautiful, shifting landscape beyond, and a place of cathartic respite. But I was also interested in maximizing the use of passive strategies for coping with the broad seasonal temperature swings, using "free" solar and wind energy.'

The building is fully self-sufficient, with its own septic tank and a well that supplies water. Electricity is provided by an eight-panel solar array on the roof of the nearby shed, which is a tiny echo of the main building. This shed also holds battery storage, a back-up generator and a propane-fed water heater that supplies the radiant underfloor heating in the house during the winter. Low-energy appliances further reduce energy needs in this tranquil retreat among fields, where nature is a continual presence. 'The constantly changing landscape gives me sunrise and sunset paintings,' says Treanor. 'There are deer passing by or grazing, and wild turkeys, raccoons and bald eagles perched high. They delight my mind and my heart.'

Opposite The timber garage and store are a simple echo of the main residence.

Above, left and right A mezzanine study and contemplation space sits above a service core, holding the partially open kitchen and the enclosed bathroom.

Right The sleeping area is at the opposite end of the house from the open-plan living area, and the service core and mezzanine are between.

Thinking Inside the Box

-

FLOAT Architectural Research and Design: Watershed,
Wren, Oregon, USA

Left Watershed can be removed and recycled at the end of its life, without any impact on the landscape.

Above Rainwater from the roof is stored in a trough that doubles as an entry step by the front door.

'The studio was designed to reveal the ecological complexity of the site ... Small tunnels under the studio bring reptiles and amphibians into view through the floor-level window and the water basin draws in birds and deer.'

Above and right The minimal furniture includes a built-in desk and shelves, while opening panels below window height offer natural ventilation.

Opposite The desk offers a framed picture of the landscape, which is all-important in the conception of this simple shelter.

The romantic ideal of the writer's cabin still has powerful resonance. Exemplified most famously by Henry David Thoreau's escapist retreat at Walden Pond, where he spent a number of years in the 1840s and produced the first drafts of *Walden, Or Life in the Woods* (1854), the notion of the creative cabin continues to enchant. It is a place of pure escapism, in which nature itself becomes the spur to original thought and imaginative pursuits. In today's fast-moving digital world, the concept of the artist's retreat, free from our countless contemporary distractions, holds sway.

Watershed is just such a retreat, commissioned by a philosopher and nature writer. This off-grid cabin is a twenty-minute drive from the town of Wren in western Oregon, and not far from the expanse of the Siuslaw National Forest. It sits in a gently sloping clearing overlooking the wetlands of Mary's River, a spellbinding setting where the sense of connection to nature is vivid and intimate, as well as inspirational.

The cabin was designed by the client's daughter, the architect Erin Moore of FLOAT, who shares her mother's interest in ecology and splices it with her work in design and construction. The two agreed that the cabin should be entirely off-grid and that it should have as little impact as possible on its surroundings. More than that, the structure should be capable of being removed and recycled at the end of its useful life, leaving little or no trace.

Another consideration was the remoteness of the setting, which has no road access. The construction process began by setting four simple concrete piers into the gentle gradient. A front-loaded off-road truck then delivered a prefabricated steel frame that was dropped on to the concrete pillars and fixed in place. Cedar wall panels were bolted to the frame, enclosing the cabin and offering glazed apertures or lenses focused on the view. Louvred panels ventilate the structure.

An important element in the 9-square-metre (100-square-foot) cabin is the fitted writing desk that faces the views across the clearing to the woodland beyond. Oil lamps and candles provide the only artificial light. A key request from the client was for a roof that would allow her to hear the rain falling; the end result, a roof made from polycarbonate, not only allows for this but also collects water, directing it into a trough alongside, which is also a doorstep.

'The studio was designed to reveal the ecological complexity of the site,' says Moore. 'Small tunnels under the studio bring reptiles and amphibians into view through the floor-level window, and the water basin draws in birds and deer. The silhouettes of these animals reflect from the water on to the interior ceiling, and windows on the west and north sides frame different bird habitats, such as the tops of the trees and the patch of sky on a hilltop updraught.'

Communal Cabins
by the Bay

-

Reiulf Ramstad Arkitekter:
Micro Cluster Cabins, Herfell, Vestfold, Norway

Opposite This second home is composed of a triptych of pine-clad pavilions.

Below The principal cabin offers wide views of the bay – a crucial part of the character and appeal of the setting.

Countryside and Forest

Right A small hut nearby, serving as a wood store, forms an echo of the main building.

Opposite The central pavilion is a communal hub, holding the principal living spaces. Bedrooms are in the cabins on either side, which can be isolated as needed.

A key element in the push towards greener and more sustainable homes is scale, since a small, well-insulated house requires far less energy and resources, in every respect, than a large one. There is an impetus among progressive architects, such as Reiulf Ramstad in Oslo, to distil the programme of a project to its essence and to encourage clients to consider with greater care the amount of enclosed living space they might truly need. 'If you persuade your client to build half of their original programme, you have done something that is unbeatable in terms of sustainability,' says Ramstad. 'It's not an easy thing to measure, but it is part of an architect's work. It's about creating a more compressed plan.'

Such an approach lay behind the design of the Micro Cluster Cabins on a site overlooking the bay of Herfellbukta, close to the southern approaches of the Oslo Fjord. Ramstad's clients wanted a weekend and holiday home that would also accommodate their grown-up children and their grandchildren. Considering how to craft a multigenerational home with low energy consumption, Ramstad decided on a flexible arrangement of three interrelated pavilions.

The central cabin features a triple-glazed façade looking south, drawing in natural warmth from the sun. This is an open-plan 'communal' hub, with areas for seating and dining, as well as a galley kitchen. The two sleeping cabins on either side can be isolated and used only as required, thereby reducing the overall energy consumption of the house. One of these cabins can be accessed directly from the hub; the other has a separate entrance, for greater privacy.

The cabins are clad in local pine, as is a small hut nearby, which serves as a wood store but also encloses a courtyard space between the rear of the cabins and a stone cliff. 'The cliff helps to shelter the house, and on sunny days the rock heats up with the sunshine and radiates heat around the house in the evenings,' says Ramstad. 'So there's an interaction between architecture and nature that adds to the comfort of the experience.'

A wood-burning stove in the hub is the main source of heating for the heavily insulated building, while the minimal electricity needs are met by local renewable power; in Norway more than 95 per cent of electricity is from renewables, mostly hydroelectricity. The house has proved such a success with its owners that they have since downsized their home in the city, reducing their footprint even further.

Opposite The interiors are made from sustainable local timber, and attics offer platforms for sleeping or storage.

Above Glazing gives edited views of the landscape, including countryside and coast.

Crafting New from Old

-

Ryall Sheridan Architects: Long Island Sound House,
Orient, Long Island, New York, USA

Opposite The house has a substantial screened porch, offering a halfway point between outdoors and in.

Above Reclaimed timber cladding adds character and texture to the façade.

The push towards energy-efficiency and renewable generation has given rise to a number of variations on the independence provided by purely off-grid living. Net zero houses, in particular, offer a model for eco-conscious living in which the overall amount of energy produced on the site outweighs that required from the grid at peak times of unusually high energy use, such as during the winter. Such houses require a connection to the grid if this system of exchange is to work, and such a link is still a planning requirement in certain districts and towns.

The net zero model applies to this house near the town of Orient, on the North Fork of Long Island, designed by Ryall Sheridan Architects. The project involved the reinvention of a modest 1970s home on a bluff overlooking Long Island Sound, for clients who also requested a new, separate painting studio. The architects were guided by Passivhaus energy efficiency standards, aiming to create two complementary, heavily insulated structures with a minimal ecological footprint.

'The clients wanted to be exposed to the views of the Sound, but they also wanted to feel comfortable and contained in their home,' says the architect William Ryall. 'They are sensitive to cold, so a warm and draught-free house was an important requirement,

while the artist's studio had to have northern light and be a flexible, open volume. We wanted to explore the use of innovative materials such as intelligent airtight membranes and triple-glazed windows, as well as mechanical systems such as the energy-recovery ventilator.'

Reclaimed cedar clads both buildings, forming a rain screen around a watertight membrane and layers of insulation, while the interior joinery is in birch plywood. The main cottage is dominated by its ground-floor living spaces, a fluid arrangement of interconnected rooms with the kitchen and dining area flowing into a screened porch. The master suite is above, and a modest lower ground floor, created by tucking the house into the gradient of the gently sloping site, contains a guest bedroom.

The house has its own well and private septic field. The main source of electricity is solar panels on the roof, while heat is provided by a wood-burning stove in the living room. Working with the heat-recovery system, the photovoltaic panels produce more than enough electricity during the summer, and this excess energy is sold back to the grid. During the coldest times of the year, additional electricity can be drawn back as required. In effect, the building uses the grid to store energy in a net zero loop. Fast-moving improvements in home battery storage are making it increasingly viable to store excess energy on the site, allowing fully off-grid variations on this model.

Opposite The main living spaces are largely open-plan, with the master bedroom on an upper storey and a guest bedroom on the lower ground floor.

Left Seen from the living area, the screened porch has the feel of a tree house.

Below Heating is provided by a wood-burning stove and a heat-recovery system.

A Nordic Island Summerhouse

—

Tham & Videgård Arkitekter: House Husarö,
Stockholm Archipelago, Sweden

Opposite From the entrance, an important sight line leads through the house to the view beyond.

Above and overleaf The folded sheet-metal cladding creates a sculptural presence against the woodland backdrop.

Left and below Vaulted ceilings lend character to the interior and soften the linear outline of the house. Splashes of colour stand out against a neutral, organic palette of materials.

Opposite The upper floor contains a master bedroom and a bunkroom; the wall panels are of wood fibreboard.

The energy needs of a home are dictated by the way it is used, as well as the way it is designed and built. The long tradition of Nordic summerhouses and cabins has been built up around the notion of simple, low-maintenance retreats solely for use in the kinder, warmer months of the year, and most – especially the more remote – lack mains services. This tradition continues in countries such as Sweden, where a new generation of twenty-first-century cabins and isolated escapes has a powerful allure.

This summer retreat by Tham & Videgård is on one of the more remote islands at the outer edges of the Stockholm archipelago, accessible only by boat; scheduled ferry services take about two and a half hours from the city itself. The cottage sits in a clearing of pine trees, on a high position looking out across the water, a short walk from a private dock.

'The property has been in the client's family for a long time,' says the architect Martin Videgård, 'and there are a couple of complementary buildings – a boathouse and a guest house. As the family has grown with each generation, the need for a larger house with more space has followed.'

The design of the summerhouse was strongly influenced by the context, in every sense. It responds to its setting, but was partly shaped by the need to bring in materials – and manpower – by boat, and by its relatively modest budget. The framework of the house is of glue-laminated wooden beams, and plywood and wood fibreboard are used internally. The outer shell is of folded sheet metal with a black finish, echoing the pitch-coated boathouses and fishermen's huts that are found across the region, but in a clearly contemporary form.

The lower level is largely open-plan, with a galley kitchen to one side of a service core holding a bathroom and storage. The rest of this fluid living space (with areas for seating and dining) revolves around the views of the shore, framed by a wall of glass and a vaulted timber ceiling. Upstairs are a bedroom and a children's bunkroom/playroom.

The sole source of heating for the entire house is a wood-burning stove on the ground floor, while ventilation relies on natural cooling. Lighting is electric (mostly from renewable sources in this part of Sweden), but during the long summer days the demand is minimal, especially given the quality of natural light in the house. The building shares a private water source with neighbours, and has its own septic system. 'It is more or less net zero, as the only heating is the fireplace,' says Videgård. 'Since it's used only in the summer, no heating is really needed, and it is also more or less maintenance-free thanks to the metal cladding.'

A Victorian Retreat on the Ridge

-

Wolveridge Architects: Hill Plains House,
Victoria, Australia

The architect Jerry Wolveridge has found a very special spot to make a new home for himself and his family. His Hill Plains House sits on a ridge not far from the picturesque gold-rush town of Kyneton, in a region famous for its wineries and vineyards. The house looks across a gentle landscape that is almost English in feel during the green spring, before the summer sun starts to bleach the countryside. In the distance lie Mount Macedon and the foothills of the Great Dividing Range, while eagles, cockatoos, rainbow lorikeets and other birds enjoy the quiet of this rural spot about an hour's drive north of Melbourne, where Wolveridge has his architectural practice.

Given the contours of the land and the woods that line the approach road, the house truly reveals itself only once you pull into the drive and begin to make your way towards it, just as the gently undulating countryside also comes into view. The single-storey house draws inspiration from the region's farmhouses, barns and sheds, although its outline and form are distinctly contemporary.

The exterior skin of the house is made from recycled blackbutt timber, pierced by large picture windows. A front porch is partially clad in a non-reflective, smoked-charcoal glass, which is repeated on the protruding shower block at the back of the house, complete with a large window that frames a view of a landmark spotted gum tree.

The interiors evolved gradually, with a number of contributions from Wolveridge's wife, Christina Theodorou, who is also an architect. At the centre is an open-plan living area, including the kitchen, with banks of floor-to-ceiling windows front and back. Floors are of polished concrete and the high ceilings are of blackbutt. Many elements were designed specially, including the kitchen island, which has the feel of a rustic workbench. The dramatic, textured wall to one side, which holds the fireplace as well as disguising a galley study beyond, was crafted from a vast collection of recycled timber blocks. The master suite is at the opposite end of the house.

The central service spine contains the shower room and a utility space, complete with a wood-burning stove that is used to heat water for a hydronic heating panel system in the winter; everyday hot water is provided by a roof-mounted solar system. Being completely off-grid, the house has a 4.6-kilowatt photovoltaic array, also on the roof, to provide electricity, in combination with battery storage. Rainwater is harvested and stored for domestic use in an underground tank, with any overflow running into a nearby dam; extra water needed for the garden can be drawn up from a well by the windmill on the brow of the hill.

'Because we are quite elevated here, we do get a huge amount of bird life passing through,' says Wolveridge. 'There's this plant called onion weed that grows wild among the grass here, and when the cockatoos get on to it they will come in their thousands and hoe the ground getting it out. We have swallows in the garage and a couple of turtles in the dam, and the kangaroo life is quite incredible. We back on to a state forest, so they start making their way out of the forest around four in the afternoon and come into the open. It's really special.'

'We have swallows in the garage and a couple of turtles in the dam, and the kangaroo life is quite incredible. It's really special.'

Previous pages and opposite The house's setting is enticing, on the brow of a ridge that offers panoramic views.

Above A sheltered vegetable garden sits to one side of the house, and there is an outdoor dining area to the rear.

Right Wood for the fireplace dries in the entrance lobby, which frames a far-reaching view of the countryside.

Above The living areas are open-plan, so that the kitchen and dining room are in the same space as the seating gathered around the fireplace.

Right Rooms such as the master bathroom are practical but also elegant, possessed of a modern yet rustic aesthetic.

Opposite The dramatic fire surround, which also screens the spaces beyond, was made from individual blocks of recycled timber, stacked on top of one another.

Portable Island Living

-

JeanArch: 72H Cabin,
Henriksholm, Dalsland, Götaland, Sweden

The cabins are independent, sculptural objects in the landscape, with few of the usual trappings of domesticity.

The cabins have a temporary quality and can be removed without leaving any impact on the landscape. They are sleeping platforms but also belvederes in miniature, framing views of sky, trees and water.

'It is extraordinarily beautiful here, and nature is unusually varied on the island. There are high hills, beautiful forests and fields of flowers. The water in the lake is clean enough to drink.'

The architect Jeanna Berger spent her childhood summers on the tranquil island of Henriksholm, to the north of Gothenburg in southern Sweden. The island, which is partly owned by her family, is accessible only by boat and sits in the clear waters of Lake Ånimmen. It is a picturesque setting for an escape into natural living.

'It is extraordinarily beautiful here, and nature is unusually varied on the island,' says Berger. 'There are high hills, beautiful forests and fields of flowers, and highland cattle, roe deer, badgers, foxes and birds are the island's only permanent residents. The water in the lake is clean enough to drink, and there are plenty of fish.'

Berger's family have had a country house on the 100-hectare (250-acre) island for many years, and also own a quartet of rental cabins nearby. The island recently became the setting for a very different kind of residence, designed by Berger, known as the 72-hour Cabin. Five of these lightweight, semi-transparent, off-grid cabins have been built for use by visitors for a few days at a time.

The cabins were designed with a simple, manageable set of component parts that could be taken to the island by boat and carried to their sites. The framework, doors and end wall are made of local spruce, as is the platform floor, which hovers above the ground on simple wooden legs. The sides and roof of the cabin are fitted with panels of Lexan – a kind of clear, light Plexiglas.

The transparency of the cabins provides a vivid and immediate sense of connection with the surrounding woodland landscape, as well as views of the lake. Inside, a bed has the timber gable end as its headboard. Lighting is provided by candle lanterns, and there is no electricity. Water comes directly from the lake and composting toilets are hidden discreetly among the trees; food is provided to order and can be heated on an open fire. The cabins were constructed without causing damage of any kind to their settings, and can be easily dismantled and removed when they come to the end of their useful lives.

With such deliberately minimal facilities and services, the intention is to encourage residents to live outside as much as possible, enjoying the privacy of the island and retreating to the cabin for quiet contemplation or rest. The buildings also function as observatories, forming simple belvederes for watching the trees, the water and the night sky.

'I see these buildings as tiny chapels devoted to nature and contemplation of our role within it,' says Berger. 'The footprint was kept small to remind the inhabitant of his or her role in the natural world. Our relationship with nature should be more humble, and we, as humans, tend to feel untouchable when we live in large buildings and cities. The intention is to help repair this relationship with nature. The small living area of the cabins forces you to bring your activities outside.'

Hillside
and Mountains

The decision to go off-grid can be very liberating. Instead of worrying about how to connect to utilities and existing services, with all of the compromises and restrictions that this can involve, the challenge lies in creating a comfortable level of self-sufficiency and independence. This, in turn, generally leads to a focus on green energy, such as wood-burning stoves for heating, using timber from sustainable sources. The technology of photovoltaics has advanced rapidly in recent years, and the cost has fallen, making solar power an obvious option for generating electricity. Add the possibilities of wind power, home hydro and private water sources, such as wells or rainwater harvesting, and off-grid living can now practically offer an important level of freedom when it comes to where we choose to make our homes.

Environments and settings that might have seemed too extreme for twenty-first-century living have therefore become tempting possibilities. This is especially true of remote, isolated and high-altitude locations, where grid-based services are unlikely to be available. Hillsides and mountains, where tranquility and open views are an essential part of the allure, become more realistic options for one-off houses with a minimal footprint and a deeply rooted respect for the environment.

These are cabins and rural retreats that demand a considered and thoughtful response to the natural world, particularly in relation to extremes of temperature and harsh weather. Hillside and mountain escapes require a particular focus on design strategies – both passive and active – that are highly contextual.

DUST's Casa Caldera (see page 98), for instance, high in a desert in Arizona, is an off-grid home that had to be able to cope with strong fluctuations in temperature between day, night and the changing seasons. Its architect, Cade Hayes, compares the interactivity required from the owner of the house to the process of sailing a boat, given that constant attention and adjustment are required to cool the house by opening windows and the central breezeway, or to warm it by closing those apertures and lighting the fireplace and stove.

The extremes can be intense, as we see with Jarmund Vigsnæs' off-grid Rabot Cabin (see page 104), on one of the tallest mountain ranges in northern Norway. This refuge – used by mountaineers and hikers – also requires effort and engagement from its residents, who must light and manage the wood-burning stoves for heating and pump water manually from a nearby lake.

Such interaction fosters a close relationship not just with the building but also with nature itself. The architects David and Susan Scott built their off-grid Alpine Cabin on Vancouver Island (see page 130) to encourage just such a sense of connection in their own family. Their way of life there, warmed by a stove and lit by candlelight, is shaped by the pattern of daylight, the changes in the weather and the character of the seasons. Every autumn the Scotts and their children begin the process of readying the cabin for the winter ski season and squirrelling away firewood.

Similarly, the architect Jesse Garlick of PLATFORM Architecture + Design created the Sky House (see page 124) on a hilltop in Washington state as a self-built home for himself and his partner, demanding vital engagement not just in the construction process but also in the day-to-day 'management' of the house and

its natural resources. The rewards, of course, are clear to see: the house is in an astonishing setting, looking out over a vast panorama of undulating hills and valleys.

For many, this kind of conscious engagement with the daily 'management' of the home and, through it, a more direct relationship with the natural world and the changing seasons is a key part of the impetus to go off-grid. The owners of Camp Baird (see page 92), in California's Sonoma County, wanted to replicate a kind of upscale camping experience with 'physical comfort but minimal luxury'. The design of their cabin, by the architect Malcolm Davis, deliberately pulls the family outside whenever possible, with features such as an open-air shower and an outdoor fireplace and cooking spot on the veranda. The refinement of finishes and fittings inside the house is, accordingly, modest and minimal, and the landscape around it has been preserved and respected as far as possible.

Anyone living or spending time in such remote and naturally beautiful settings has a guardianship role in terms of conservation. Landscaping tends to be kept to a minimum, and the house itself forms the lightest possible presence on the land, with minimal disturbance. FLOAT's Outside House (see page 114) on a slope in Maui, Hawaii, for example, is little more than two platforms floating above the hillside.

Any landscaping or planting that was required for the houses in these pages has been handled with great sensitivity, by introducing or replanting native species that are suited to the natural conditions of the setting, and by using harvested rainwater for irrigation. For example, the architect Renée del Gaudio and her husband built their home in a canyon landscape near Boulder, Colorado, to replace a small cabin that was lost in a devastating wildfire. She and her family have supported and encouraged fresh planting around the Sunshine Canyon House (see page 110), but only with indigenous trees and shrubs that are suited to the climate.

The owners of the House in Extremadura, Spain (see page 86), have also shown respect for the green landscape around their home in the hills. The project involved the replacement of an old stables in an isolated rural setting with a new, off-grid house by ÁBATON Arquitectura. With no option to connect to grid services, the family were able to make the most of the mountain streams, drawing on them not only for water but also to generate hydroelectricity using small turbines. In doing so, they were able to use the natural resources of the hills while protecting and preserving the local environment.

Remote Mountain Vistas

-

ÁBATON Arquitectura: House in Extremadura,
Cáceres, Extremadura, Spain

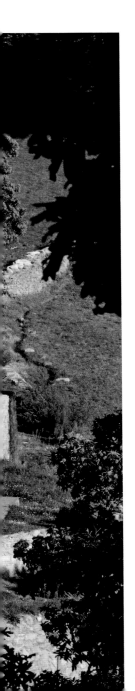

The house seeks to connect with its surroundings via large apertures, including the barn door to one side, which opens to reveal bedrooms on two levels.

87

Sometimes the decision to go off-grid is driven by necessity as much as by good intentions. That was the case with the House in Extremadura by ÁBATON Arquitectura. In this remote area of hills, high sierra and forest without mains services of any kind, the only option was to go off-grid and find sustainable sources of water and energy. The architects and their client chose small-scale hydroelectricity generation using turbine systems in the local water courses, fed by rainwater running off the hills.

The house is in the district of Cáceres, an area of rugged landscape, nature reserves and national parks about two thirds of the way from Madrid to the Portuguese border. 'The environment is unique,' says Camino Alonso of the Madrid-based practice. 'The house is in a remote place on top of the mountains with views of this beautiful valley. We filter water from the streams to use as tap water, and we have solar panels plus turbines in the river to provide the required energy. It is completely off-grid. We just have an emergency generator in case the energy systems fail.'

The architect's clients bought an abandoned stable in the hope of converting it to residential use, but the stable was ultimately found to be in such poor condition that it made better sense to build a house from scratch on the same site, using recycled local stone and indigenous materials. 'We wanted to respect the original architecture of the stables but also provide a modern space inside,' says Alonso. 'The result looks traditional from the outside but contrasts with the contemporary interiors. We also wanted the house to appear quite small from the surrounding countryside but feel very spacious inside. The huge windows to the front, open to the landscape, helped us to achieve both goals.'

The house sits sensitively and naturally on the gently sloping hillside, adopting much the same profile as the old stables. Towards the front is a long, open living area, with zones for seating and dining arranged around two wood-burning fireplaces. This area leads out to the adjoining terrace through large apertures in the façade, which can be sealed by both glazing and barn-style timber doors and shutters. Two bedrooms are on the lower level, towards the back, and two more, plus a bunkroom, are on a mezzanine above.

Water is a repeated theme throughout. A secret courtyard between the back of the house and a retaining wall to the hillside holds a sculptural sequence of pools, while the simple swimming pool at the front of the house doubles as a holding tank for irrigation and is also fed by the local streams. The house has its own waste-water treatment plant, which requires emptying every five years. The building's approach to the landscape and its resources is truly symbiotic.

Opposite The living space at the front of the house connects with views of the valley and woodland.

Right Bedrooms are towards the back of the house, over two floors, connecting to the outdoors via side windows and doors.

Below, left and right A mezzanine floats over the living spaces; the gap between the back of the house and the hill acts as a light well, while also holding pools and planting.

Hillside and Mountains

Below Newly built but using local, reclaimed stone, the house adapts itself to the shape of the hillside and sits discreetly in the landscape.

Opposite The dining area features a long communal table and looks out onto the adjoining terrace.

'The environment is
unique. The house is in
a remote place on top of
the mountains with views
of this beautiful valley.'

The Indoor–Outdoor Experience

-

Malcolm Davis Architecture: Camp Baird,
Healdsburg, California, USA

Opposite, above and overleaf The spacious
veranda and screened porch are essential
components, forming transitional spaces
between outdoors and in.

The owners of Camp Baird first got to know the area around Healdsburg, in the wine region of Sonoma County, on family hiking trips. Immersing themselves in the woods of the region and the experience of outdoor living, they decided to try to replicate these pleasures in the design of their home there, set among 67 hectares (165 acres) of oak and bay trees. Sitting within a clearing in the hills, the weekend and holiday house designed by the architect Malcolm Davis was founded on the idea of camping, with a wealth of open-air spaces, including an outdoor fireplace on the veranda and an outside shower. It was also vital to the clients, both of whom are committed environmentalists, that the house be fully off-grid.

'It was a core component of the project,' say Davis's clients, who have two daughters and whose main house was also designed by the architect. 'We could have chosen to run power lines to hook into the local grid, but the distance of that run and the impact on the land made it unpalatable. We are completely self-sufficient here and we wanted a house that would be outdoors-focused, where we wouldn't find ourselves sitting inside when we were immersed in this incredible setting. We wanted physical comfort but minimal luxury.'

Davis developed a plan for a compound in the woods that encapsulated many of the greatest delights of outdoor living, with an emphasis on halfway spaces between inside and out. The cabin itself has a large veranda and a screened porch, from where the family can look out across the solar-heated swimming pool to the countryside beyond.

'The notion of the porch figures largely in my work,' says Davis. 'The structure of the house is really a series of layers, from fully enclosed spaces to roofed and screened spaces and then only roofed, before reaching the exposed decks around the pool. The elemental materials and simple forms are evocative of vernacular rural structures, but the building has been refined to create the epitome of casual indoor-outdoor living in a remote landscape.'

The pavilion-like house has a central entry hall that doubles as a breezeway and connects directly with the kitchen and porch, which is used principally for dining with a view. The three other rooms at either end of the pavilion are simple, multifunctional spaces for sleeping, yoga or exercising. This simplicity is deliberate, intended to refocus attention on open-air living. A separate shed holds garaging, a workshop and storage.

Heating is provided by wood-burning stoves, while electricity comes from an array of solar panels nearby; a solar thermal system heats hot water for domestic use and for the pool, as required. All appliances were chosen for their low energy consumption, while cooling is provided naturally and a back-up generator kicks in only in case of problems elsewhere. The planting around the house was selected for its modest water requirements and its resistance to drought.

'We like the fact that the house affords us comfort in a beautiful environment while compelling us to spend nearly every waking hour outdoors,' says the family. 'We have expansive views of the valley, and for most of the year we can hear the sound of the nearby creeks. Many mornings we awake to a beautiful sunrise overlooking the fog-filled valley and enjoy our morning coffee watching the fog slowly lifting and burning off. It's a very dynamic yet peaceful experience.'

Opposite The cabin sits gently in the landscape, nestled in a natural dip in the hills.

Above, left The main entrance doubles as a breezeway at the centre of the house, drawing cool air through the building.

Above and left Simple indoor amenities are complemented by outdoor alternatives, such as this open-air shower fed by water from the site.

Creating a Desert Oasis

-

DUST: Casa Caldera,
San Rafael Valley, Arizona, USA

The simple form of the house, which is made of lava concrete, allows it to sit low in the landscape, softened by desert bushes and planting.

Casa Caldera takes its name from the volcanic landscape of this particular part of Arizona, which was formed by volcanic craters known as calderas. It also refers to the earthy blocks used to build the single-storey house, made of scoria (lava concrete), in which volcanic cinder is an important ingredient. The blocks help the house to blend into its remote setting on a former ranch in the San Rafael Valley, about two hours' drive south of Tucson and not far from the Mexican border. The isolation of the site, which is accessible only via long dirt roads and is nearly 2 kilometres (about 1 mile) from the nearest neighbour, meant the decision to go off-grid was a natural one.

'This project really forced us to get real with human comfort, including passive cooling and thermal performance,' says the architect, Cade Hayes of DUST. 'It deepened our understanding of how to live in a home that responds to the diurnal temperature swings and the microclimate. But the house does not respond alone, and our client has to engage with it, essentially "sailing" it by opening it up or closing it down, or using wood and fire to control the heating and cooling.'

DUST's client asked for a modest and self-sufficient home that could be locked down and secured when not in use, and that would blend in with the cinematic high desert landscape, which sits at an elevation of about 1,500 metres (5,000 feet). The architect was inspired by traditional Spanish Colonial zaguán houses, creating a

small, modern variant on buildings defined by a long central hallway. Here, the wooden gates that secure the zaguán can be opened at either end to create a central breezeway that runs through the house and doubles as a kind of sheltered porch. This open corridor plays a vital part in ventilating the house naturally during the day, allowing the breeze to spill into the open-plan living room and dining/kitchen area to one side (behind an internal wall of glass) and the two bedrooms to the other (behind an internal wall of sassafras timber).

The thick, insulated walls help to regulate the temperature inside the house, which totals about 93 square metres (just over 1,000 square feet). The main sources of heating for the evenings or during the cooler months are an open wood-burning fireplace in the sitting room and a compact stove in the secondary hallway between the two bedrooms. Electricity is provided by a 1.8 kilowatt solar array, and water comes from a well on the property. Rainwater collected on the roof is used to water a grove of native Emory oaks, common to the area, which shade the house, while recycled grey water from an independent septic system provides more water for vegetation; in the future the owner, a winemaker, hopes to plant vines as well.

'The user has to be in tune with the climate and the flexibility of the house,' says Hayes. 'For the client and for us the project was an ideal pursuit of an era before technology and electricity. That was our base, and we looked to solve each problem thoughtfully and carefully.'

Previous pages and opposite The central hallway acts as a breezeway, drawing in light and fresh air; bedrooms are to one side and living spaces to the other.

Below The sitting room is arranged around a fireplace, and the windows provide a framed view of the landscape.

Shelter in the High Mountains

—

Jarmund Vigsnæs: Rabot Cabin,
Okstindan, Nordland, Norway

The cabin offers high-altitude refuge in the Okstindan mountains, where the conditions are extreme and the views extraordinary.

The Rabot Cabin is named after the French explorer, glaciologist and geographer Charles Rabot. It was he who first fully explored the mountains and glaciers of the county of Nordland, Norway, in the 1880s; at about the same time, in 1883, he became the first person to climb the tallest mountain in Sweden, Kebnekaise.

Designed by the architectural practice Jarmund Vigsnæs, the cabin serves as a shelter for hikers and mountaineers in the Okstindan mountain range, which includes the peak Oksskolten, the highest point in northern Norway. In such an extreme environment self-sufficiency was essential, as was a hard-wearing, durable, low-maintenance building that could cope with sub-zero temperatures and driving snow.

'The cabin is about 1,200 metres (4,000 feet) above sea level and very close to one of the glaciers,' says the architect, Ane Sønderaal Tolfsen. 'The setting is spectacular, but the weather can be extremely harsh and there is no infrastructure. There are very few cabins or other structures at this elevation in Norway.'

The only access is on foot or by helicopter, and the latter was used to bring in all the building materials. The cabin was largely built by local volunteers, using native spruce cladding, high-performance glazing and plywood for the interior joinery.

The irregular shape of the building evolved after studies of the snowdrift patterns on the site, as well as in response to the rugged topography and the views. There was also a need for flexibility in the layout of the cabin, which can accommodate between two and thirty visitors at a time.

The rhomboid structure contains a mixture of open communal spaces and simple cellular bedrooms on the ground floor, while a mezzanine holds a larger bunkroom. The floor plan was designed so that the cabin's communal zone could be divided in two when in use by fewer visitors, reducing the need for heating, which is largely provided by two wood-burning stoves that form focal points at each side. Electricity is generated by solar panels, and water must be pumped manually from a small lake nearby. A secondary emergency hut is nearby, in case of damage that might compromise the Rabot Cabin.

'The cabin has a calm and peaceful atmosphere, and both its location and the sense of connection with its surroundings are remarkable,' says Sønderaal Tolfsen. 'It encourages people to get outside and experience nature, which inspires closer contact with and an increased respect for the environment.'

Opposite and overleaf The isolated timber-clad retreat has a high-performance shell that can cope with accumulated snow and sub-zero temperatures.

Left and below The refuge contains living and dining spaces at either end, with a kitchen in the centre. Wood-burning stoves provide heat, while water is pumped from the lake below.

Flooded with Natural Light

-

Renée del Gaudio Architecture: Sunshine Canyon House,
Boulder, Colorado, USA

The living spaces are on the *piano nobile*, which offers views of the valley and the surrounding hills and mountains.

When it comes to her family home in the hills near Boulder, Colorado, what pleases Renée del Gaudio most 'is that it feels as though it could not belong anywhere else. It's a modern interpretation of the area's vernacular architecture, but the design also seeks to establish a language of its own, specific to its context and location.'

The Sunshine Canyon House is inspired by the area's agricultural heritage and its history of mines and miner's cottages. It is clad in a protective layer of rusting Corten steel that echoes the old infrastructure of the mines, while the pitched, gabled roof is reminiscent of barns and agricultural sheds. But the house is closely tailored both to the site and to the needs of the family, while ensuring a net zero performance in terms of energy use.

Del Gaudio and her husband, Ross Wehner, had owned the plot for some years, while nursing an ambition to relocate from Denver. There had been a small cabin on the land, but it was destroyed by a fire that also claimed many of the neighbouring homes, along with the mature pines and fir trees that dotted the hills. The damage was shocking, but in time del Gaudio and her family were able to seize the opportunity to build a fresh full-time home here while also restoring and replanting the 1.8 hectares (4½ acres) of land around it.

The architect developed her ideas for a sustainable home in direct response to the natural conditions of the site and its topography,

tucking the two-storey building into the side of the hill and making the most of the wide views across the landscape towards Boulder Reservoir and the Front Range mountains. Family bedrooms are on the lower level, with porches at either end, and the main living spaces are above, making the most of the vistas and bountiful natural light. Here, an open-plan seating, dining and kitchen area leads out to a substantial deck perched above the master suite. It is warmed by solar gain through extensive triple glazing, and by a wood-burning stove when necessary. A separate guest bedroom and studio are at the far end of the house.

The house's net zero performance is achieved with a combination of passive strategies and home-grown renewable energy. The building is heavily insulated, and its design makes the most of both solar gain and natural ventilation. The main source of electricity is a 3.6 kilowatt photovoltaic array on the roof of the adjacent garage/store, while appliances and lighting were chosen for their low energy requirements. The wood-burner is fed with timber saved from the trees ravaged by the wildfire.

Fresh tree cover has now established itself, as the natural vegetation recovers. 'We reintroduced native plant species to prevent erosion and support the local wildlife,' says del Gaudio. 'Today, mountain grasses, wild flowers and the deer, foxes, birds and bears have all returned and appear to be thriving.'

Opposite The upper-storey living spaces are open-plan, with the kitchen at one end and seating at the other, separated by the dining area.

Left and below The house nestles discreetly into the hillside, with a bridge connecting the upper storey to the higher point of the slope.

Bottom A wood-burning stove is the main source of heat in this extensively insulated home, which also uses solar power.

Love of the Land

-

FLOAT Architectural Research and Design: Outside House, Maui, Hawaii

The landscapes of the Hawaiian islands are unique and
mesmerizing. Formed by a continuing process of volcanic
eruption that has pushed the isles above the surrounding
sea, they feel particularly alive. It is fascinating to see how
nature claims the harsh volcanic terrain and softens and
enriches it over time, even in the islands' active volcanic parks. It is a
place where the sense of connection to nature is both deeply rooted
and vivid.

The owner of this hillside house was born and brought up
on the Hawaiian island of Maui and lives in the town of Wailea,
which has grown in scale and stature as a tourist destination. Yet she
has always harboured fond memories of quieter times and treasured
a sense of connection to Maui's own special landscape. When she
inherited a long-standing family plot in a rural part of the island, she
was determined to follow her own interests in land conservation
and create a retreat where she could rediscover the sense of freedom
that comes from a direct and vivid relationship with the landscape.
This was the thinking behind the Outside House, where the spaces
between and around a pair of light, discreet pavilions would always
be more important than the structures themselves.

'The client is a hospice social worker and land conservationist
who uses the higher-elevation Outside House as a cool-temperature
retreat from her work and life in town,' says the architect Erin Moore
of FLOAT Architectural Research and Design. 'It was built as a

point of connection between her and the land she stewards, and the
pavilions were designed to be minimally connected to the ground,
and demountable.'

Each pavilion has a character and identity of its own. The
first is called Mauka, which translates from the Hawaiian language
as 'inland towards the mountain'. This is a simple sleeping pavilion
and studio made from a combination of western red cedar and
polycarbonate sheathing; the structure is mounted on four concrete
blocks pushed into the slope.

The second pavilion, Makai ('seaward'), is essentially a
floating, open-sided deck or platform, made of juniper wood fixed
to a lightweight steel frame. A simple protective canopy shelters a
seating area facing the views, and a simple kitchenette to the back
with shower area behind.

At present the Outside House is off-grid, but with the simplest
of facilities that one might expect from a camping experience, relying
on solar- or battery-powered lanterns and a composting toilet;
water must be brought in manually. The pavilions were designed so
that the client can add a solar array with battery storage, as well as
rainwater harvesting and grey-water recycling for irrigation. 'The
Outside House is intended to demonstrate the client's ecocentric
world view,' says Moore. 'It's a perspective that is rooted in the
Hawaiian concept of "aloha aina" – love of the land.'

'The Outside House is intended to demonstrate the client's ecocentric world view. It's a perspective that is rooted in the Hawaiian concept of "aloha aina" – love of the land.'

Previous pages and opposite The two pavilions float above the hillside, causing as little disturbance to the land as possible. The open-sided platform contains the kitchenette and a seating area facing the view.

Left and above The enclosed micro-cabin is a simple studio with space enough for sleeping, working and reading.

Perched on the Brow of the Hill

-

_naturehumaine: Bolton Residence,
Eastern Townships, Quebec, Canada

The house is an engaging viewing platform, looking
out over the valley below and the mountains beyond.

This spread and overleaf The stairs ascend from the plinth to the living spaces and master bedroom, which offer a vivid sense of connection with the landscape.

A key source of inspiration for the outline and form of this dramatic hilltop home in Quebec was the covered bridge common to the Eastern Townships region and neighbouring Vermont. The upper level of the house, which cantilevers over its smaller, subservient base, certainly has a bridge-like quality, and its sculptural form seems all the more dramatic not just for its cladding of black fibre cement boards (reminiscent of pitch-painted timber), but also for its dominant position on the brow of a hill. Here, the house makes the most of the wide views of the valley below, and of a vista northwards to Mount Orford. Establishing a vivid sense of connection to the landscape was a guiding principle for the design of this very sustainable and largely self-sufficient home.

'What makes it unique is the position of the house on the site,' says the architect Stéphane Rasselet of _naturehumaine. 'We decided to sit the new construction on a bedrock that offers views eastwards over the valley while making the least impact on the site overall. The client works in the American film industry, and at times his work can be quite intense, so he wanted a quiet and simple retreat where he could recharge his batteries. It's a small house with just a master bedroom and one additional bedroom for guests.'

The lower level forms a modestly scaled concrete plinth pushed into the slope of the hill. It holds the main entrance

(connecting with a carport), service spaces and guest accommodation, but is seldom used, apart from access, when the owner is at the house alone.

The upper storey, floating above the plinth, contains the principal living spaces of seating area, dining zone and kitchen arranged in an open-plan layout. A substantial, slow-combustion wood-burning stove anchors the space and is the main source of heat for the heavily insulated house, including the master suite alongside. The living room also flows out on to a deck above the carport.

Water comes from the house's own deep well, while waste water is treated and filtered on the site by a natural septic system. Electricity is supplied via a line from the local utility company, which generates hydroelectric power. In this respect the energy provided is wholly sustainable and renewable, rendering other options for home generation more or less redundant.

The overall footprint of the house, in terms of its physical imprint on the land and its energy requirements, is minimal. It serves as a twenty-first-century belvedere, framing engaging views of an unspoilt and open landscape. 'It has this simple form solidly anchored to its natural surroundings,' says Rasselet. 'The main idea was to create a house that gave the impression of being suspended in nature.'

Sculpted from
the Landscape

-

PLATFORM Architecture + Design: Sky House,
Oroville, Washington, USA

This spread and pages 128–29 The house was designed to have the greatest possible connection with the terrace and, beyond it, the panoramic prospect. The steel plates used for the exterior coat lend the house an abstract, sculptural and semi-industrial character.

Sitting alone on a remote hilltop in Washington state, close to the Canadian border, the Sky House has the sculptural look of a piece of land art. This small two-storey home clad in steel plates was partly inspired by the work of such modern sculptors as Richard Serra and by the abstract paintings of Mark Rothko. Over time the plates will rust further, adding to the patina of the house, which was designed by the architect Jesse Garlick as an off-grid escape for himself and his wife, Susan Elliott.

'We wanted a place to contemplate the world, take a break from the city and be outside,' says Garlick, whose practice, PLATFORM Architecture + Design, is based in Vancouver. 'The site is spectacular, on a knoll overlooking the Cascade Foothills and the central Okanagan valley. The view is like an ever-changing painting. The architecture was first and foremost about celebrating the site, and, because of the unique nature of the climate – from extreme sun to cold, snowy winters – the building had to be robust but respectful.'

The couple began by camping out on the site, living in a tent while designing and then building the house. They began with the idea of building a tiny structure, inspired by traditional log cabins, but gradually decided that they wanted a small house that would be just big enough to accommodate visiting family and friends, so that they could share the experience of immersion in this cinematic landscape.

Garlick worked on the building with his brother, a skilled carpenter, bringing in local help as needed. He decided on a structural framework of prefabricated cross-laminated timber beams and a steel shell. The materials could be brought in by truck but had to be lifted into place by hand, a fact that dictated the size and weight of each piece in the puzzle. The house was heavily insulated and positioned carefully to maximize solar gain in the winter and reduce the impact of the summer sun; it has a natural ventilation strategy for the warmer months that vents hot air from the upper windows.

The ground floor is dominated by the open-plan living area, which includes a substantial kitchen where the couple cook meals for friends and family. A run of sliding glass doors opens to the adjoining terrace, while a wood-burning stove by the seating and dining area warms the house. The ground floor also has a sleeping nook containing a daybed, sectioned off with a curtain; the mezzanine holds the master bedroom and the single bathroom.

The ambition from the start was to be fully off-grid. A small solar array next to the house provides electricity and powers a pump that draws water from a well into underground storage tanks. Propane canisters feed the cooking range and also power a back-up generator in a storage wall alongside the building, and there is a septic field for waste water. 'We were pleased that the building didn't detract from the special nature of the place,' says Garlick. 'The house has a small footprint and uses little water or electricity, so it attempts to tread lightly on the land. I feel very good about the sense of place and the experiential quality of the architecture.'

Opposite, left A mezzanine overlooking the living space holds the principal bedroom.

Opposite, right, and below The living area on the ground floor is warmed by a wood-burning stove, and a bedroom alcove to one side can be screened off with a simple sliding curtain.

Attuned to Nature's Rhythms

-

Scott & Scott Architects: Alpine Cabin,
Vancouver Island, Canada

Opposite The irregular, angled shape of the roof encourages snow to slide off rather than accumulate and become too heavy.

Below The sheltered porch doubles as a dry wood store – essential for heating the house.

A modern interpretation of a traditional timber cabin, David and Susan Scott's escapist home on Vancouver Island offers a way of living in tune with the seasons and the natural patterns of the day. The cabin is fully off-grid and thus requires a level of conscious interaction from the Scotts and their two daughters. This includes preparing the house for the autumn, including gathering timber for the wood-burning stove, and adapting to the rhythms of the light and the weather in the winter, when the cabin is used the most.

'The project isn't characterized by advanced technology but by a desire to use simple methods and enjoy the changes in temperature and light,' say the Scotts, who acted as architects, builders and clients for the Alpine Cabin. 'We were both involved in complex projects with other architectural practices at the time we began working on the cabin, and our intention was to work directly and in a free manner that was responsive to the site conditions and the available materials.'

The setting is the alpine peaks of Vancouver Island. The Scotts' parcel of land is in a quiet spot close to a community-run ski area; its remoteness means that there are no grid-based utility services of any kind, so that required a simple set of solutions to the challenge of providing heat and water.

The programme for the house was a basic one, with the aim of providing a winter escape from everyday living in Vancouver itself, just across the Strait of Georgia. A key aspect of the design of the building, in an area that can experience 1.5 metres (nearly 5 feet) of snow accumulation in a winter season, was to ensure that the roof would shed snow effectively while creating a safe and sheltered entry zone (which doubles as a dry store for firewood).

The house, which is partly raised above the slope on timber pillars, is made almost entirely of wood, with Douglas fir for the structural framework, cedar boards for the cladding and a mix of plywood and planed fir for the internal joinery.

'We built the cabin, with volunteering friends who share our equal love of making things and powder boarding,' say the Scotts. 'It was formative in our desire to start an architectural practice where we can challenge ourselves with designing and crafting work in challenging sites where adventure is the reward.'

The 100-square-metre (1,075-square-foot) cabin contains an open-plan living area on the ground floor, plus a sauna, with two bedrooms and a den upstairs; the porch is sheltered by one of the bedrooms. The stove, which burns locally collected wood, is the only source of heat, while candelabras provide light in the evenings. Water for washing and cooking must be collected manually from the nearby creek. 'For us, it's a work in progress – a place where we can go to observe the manner in which a shelter functions in the environment,' say the architects. 'But it's also very peaceful and there's an extraordinary display of stars in the night sky. Our daughters have known the cabin all their lives and it is special to share a place with them where there is no phone coverage and where the basic aspects of habitation – collecting water, creating heat and light – are a daily part of our lives.'

Opposite and below The simple, crafted interiors have built-in elements, including integrated seating, and are lit by candles.

Right As well as a wood store, the porch doubles as a boot and ski room.

'There's an extraordinary display of stars in the night sky. Our daughters have known the cabin all their lives and it is special to share a place with them where there is no phone coverage.'

Hillside and Mountains

The house is discreetly placed among the mature trees, yet it has a sculptural character of its own.

Looking Out at the Fjord

—

Stinessen Arkitektur: Cabin in the Lyngen Alps, Lyngen, Troms, Norway

Opposite and above The house looks across the fjord towards the peaks on the opposite shore. Terraces and decks form transitional spaces between inside and out.

Overleaf The master bedroom looks out on to the landscape behind the house, with an angled window framing the view.

The Lyngen Alps in northern Norway form part of an Arctic landscape where the mountains meet the sea. The highest peaks reach 1,800 metres (6,000 feet), drawing skiers and mountaineers and overlooking the waters of the Lyngen Fjord, as well as the other waterways and islands of the region. It is a remote and extraordinary setting in which to build a home such as Hagbart Kraemer and Tove Feldt's cabin, designed by the architect Snorre Stinessen, which forms a seductive response to its surroundings.

Perched on a shoreside bluff, the single-storey house offers a powerful vantage point looking out across the water and towards a range of snow-capped peaks. Both architect and clients wanted to preserve the natural beauty of the landscape as far as possible, and to create this crafted observation post without damaging the environment.

'Here in the north of Norway the vegetation is particularly vulnerable,' says Stinessen. 'Any natural growth that is harmed could take years to recover, so the particular position was chosen in an area with a natural shelf, where we would have minimal impact on the landscape but also capture the panoramic views. We wanted to explore the relationship with the natural surroundings and create a balance between the views over the water and the dramatic alpine scenery on the other side.'

The cabin perches gently on the land, adapting to the shifting gradient. The spaces to the back of the house include the entrance and bedrooms, and the master suite projects at an angle to capture a specific view of the mountains. The main living spaces are in an open-plan formation to the front, facing the water, where a wall of floor-to-ceiling glass opens to a balcony that floats above the slope on slender piloti. A separate miniature cabin nearby contains a sauna. The exterior of the house, including the roof, is clad in cedar, and the interior joinery is oak. These natural materials lend a degree of organic warmth, but the cedar in particular was also chosen for its stability and durability in this extreme climate.

The house is almost self-sufficient. Heating is provided by a combination of a wood-burning stove in the living room and geothermal energy from a ground-source heat pump, which feeds an underfloor heating system and also provides hot water for domestic use. Water comes from the site, and the cabin also has a waste-water treatment system. A small amount of renewable power comes from locally generated hydroelectricity, forming the only link to local utilities.

'We wanted the house to be largely independent from the energy suppliers,' say Kraemer and Feldt, who use it mainly for holidays and weekend visits. 'But we also wanted easy connections to the outdoors, and the fantastic views over the landscape make the house very special.'

Opposite The living spaces are open-plan, with floor-to-ceiling banks of glass opening to the balcony and the view.

Right The cedar cladding has turned to a soft grey, and the house's low presence echoes the rock formations along the coast.

Below, left and right Oak is used extensively inside for walls, floors and ceilings, as seen in the master bedroom, with its angled window looking out across the countryside.

Harlequin Chic in the Peaks

-

Sparano + Mooney Architecture: Emigration Canyon Residence, Utah, USA

'The rugged materials reference the landscape of the American West and hark back to the Western vernacular buildings of the region, but they also blend seamlessly into the landscape.'

Previous pages The Corten steel shingles that clad the home lend it character and echo the timber shingles used on vernacular buildings and farmsteads in the area.

Above The living spaces on the upper floor offer a vivid connection with the landscape, including the mountains all around.

Right A wood-burning fireplace is a crucial source of heat for the main part of the house, supplemented by underfloor heating.

Opposite The open-plan living area serves many purposes. The dining area at the far end doubles as a study and library, with a wall of books to one side.

Clad in a harlequin pattern of rusting, recycled Corten steel shingles, the exterior of the Emigration Canyon Residence has an earthy patina that sits well in its rugged context of hills and peaks. Corten is a material that manages to look both industrial and organic, and that has led to its increased use in many different settings. It is also hard-wearing and low-maintenance, which makes it suitable for climates where temperatures vary widely across the seasons, as is the case in this part of Utah.

'The rugged materials reference the landscape of the American West and hark back to the Western vernacular buildings of the region, but they also blend seamlessly into the landscape,' say the architects and occupants of the house, John Sparano and Anne Mooney. 'The key properties we wanted from the project were sustainability, maintainability and adaptability, with a flexible home that reflects the ever-changing quality of family life.'

The house is to the east of Salt Lake City, on a historic mountain pass that was once used by the early settlers heading west; there are high peaks to either side, with extensive ski areas to the south. The modestly sized building sits naturally in the terrain and was positioned carefully, not just to take advantage of the movement of the sun and connection with views, but also with the intention of causing minimal disturbance to the plants and shrubs on the site.

All the principal living spaces are on the top floor of the heavily insulated, triple-glazed home, enjoying a vivid sense of connection with the landscape. 'We love looking out on to the mountains and being connected to nature and the changing seasons,' say Sparano and Mooney. 'We love to open the wall of windows in the living room and experience the outdoors from within.' A discreet lower level, partly tucked into the topography of the land, forms a plinth for the building and holds service spaces as well as a flexible area that can be a playroom for Sparano and Mooney's two daughters or a guest room for visitors.

From the beginning of the project, the couple placed the emphasis on sustainability and low energy consumption. The design of the house incorporates a range of passive strategies with these goals in mind, including solar gain for the winter and natural cross-ventilation in the summer. As well as the extensive glazing, solar tubes collect and direct daylight into darker parts of the house, reducing the need for artificial lighting.

The main living spaces are warmed by a wood-burning fire in combination with zoned underfloor heating fed by a high-efficiency boiler. The house has been wired in preparation for a solar array, which will be installed by the family as soon as the budget allows, to create a net zero home. The house was the first in Utah to be awarded a LEED (Leadership in Energy and Environmental Design) for Homes silver rating. The emphasis on adaptability also ensures that the house will serve the needs of the family in a range of future circumstances.

'We love looking out on to the mountains and being connected to nature and the changing seasons. We love to open the wall of windows in the living room and experience the outdoors from within.'

The raw, earthy quality of the cladding helps to tie the house to the mountains, which are similarly raw and dramatic.

Contemporary Cottage on a Lavender Hillside

-

Studio Joseph: Small House in an Olive Grove,
Geyserville, California, USA

The zinc panels that clad the guest cottage set the tone for the interior colour palette, with its textural greys and off-whites.

Hillside and Mountains

Right Although compact, the house offers integrated outdoor rooms and open-air retreats.

Below The sitting room is an open volume, with high ceilings and large windows allowing wide views.

Opposite Even small spaces, such as the bathroom, seek a vibrant relationship with the vineyard surroundings.

Architect Wendy Joseph manages to achieve a great deal with small spaces. Here, in a rural quarter of Sonoma County, she has created a compact residence in miniature with a distinctly contemporary form that offers a direct and seductive connection with the landscape. The project echoes one of Joseph's best-known projects – a small and crafted retreat, The Writer's Studio, which is set in a forest clearing in upstate New York. This, too, was modest in scale but large in character, providing a crisp, modern building set in the woods and heated by a fireplace using wood sourced on the grounds of the property.

Small House in an Olive Grove is situated on a farm in the wine-growing district of Sonoma County, north of San Francisco. It is part of a larger project, in which Joseph also reinvented an existing house on the property as a principal residence for her Californian clients. The Small House is a new guest lodge for visiting friends and family, set on a hillside blanketed with lavender.

'We bought the property because we loved this area of Sonoma and the great views,' say the owners of the farm. 'We wanted a place that would support our agricultural ideals and where we could make great honey and olive oil to sell to local restaurants.

As part of our dedication to the land we also want to make the farm as sustainable as possible and have it function off the grid.'

As part of the overall project, the infrastructure of the property was not merely improved but transformed to create a self-sufficient farm. A solar array was installed in a field to provide all the power and heating needs for the farm as a whole, including the main residence and the guest house; the capacity of this solar field was later doubled. Water also comes from the site.

The Small House is pushed into the hillside, and inside the spaces also step up, from the living room at the lower level – looking out across the olive groves – to a mezzanine kitchen. A spur alongside contains one bedroom. A series of terraces create various outdoor rooms around it, enhancing its relationship with the surrounding plantation and woodland.

Clad in zinc panels and redwood screens, the Small House has a sculptural quality all its own. It can be opened up to allow natural cross-ventilation, in keeping with the principles of sustainability that guide the whole farm. 'The house is completely integrated into the setting,' say Joseph's clients. 'It is so open and beautiful, with huge views of the vineyards, olive trees and rolling hills. The Small House sits right in the middle of things, and as you look out it seems as though the beauty never ends.'

'The setting is ... so open and beautiful with huge views of the vineyards, olive trees and the rolling hills. The Small House sits right in the middle of things, and as you look out it seems as though the beauty never ends.'

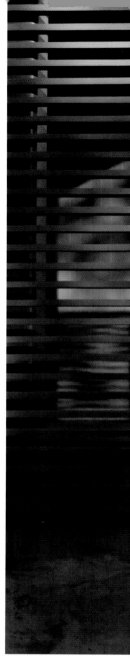

Stepping down the hillside, the house has a series of decks and terraces to the front and sides, offering a choice of outdoor 'rooms'.

Immersed in the Wilderness

—

Taalman Architecture: Clear Lake It House,
Clear Lake, California, USA

Opposite The interiors make good use of reclaimed and recycled materials, including the floors and kitchen counter.

Above The house sits on a slightly raised platform, creating a level site on which to build and also offering protection from termites.

'It's very much about living in nature. Each view has its own personality, and varies according to the time of day and the season.'

Above and right The platform that holds the house has an integrated deck that is used as an outdoor living space, but also doubles as the entry zone.

Opposite A desk in one corner of the open-plan living space is surrounded by glass walls, allowing constant connection with the mountainous setting.

This off-grid residence was commissioned by the lighting designer Terry Ohm in a ruggedly mountainous part of California, north of San Francisco, near the Mendocino National Forest. The house was built using the 'It House' prefabricated steel-framed building system developed by Taalman Architecture, which features factory made modules, and sits upon a floating platform 1.2 metres (4 feet) off the ground, helping to protect the house from termites and offering a well-insulated base. The isolated site, up a long dirt track and 4 kilometres (2½ miles) from the nearest neighbour, lent itself to a prefab construction system that limited time and labour on the site.

The basic It House system was adapted for Ohm, who was intimately involved in the design and construction. 'With the sloping mountain site we always anticipated that the house would be on a platform,' says Linda Taalman. 'Originally we thought of using wood, and then we changed to steel, and that is part of the identity of the It Cabin. Terry's house played a big part in the development of the whole It Cabin concept, and Terry himself brought many things to the table. It was a smooth process and faster than some other It projects, even though the site is very challenging to get to.'

Ohm used to live in San Francisco, and he spent a couple of years hunting for the right spot to build his country cabin before settling on Clear Lake. Given the remote location, the house had to be entirely self-sufficient; it has its own well and storage tanks for water, plus solar power and a private septic system, and natural cross-ventilation cools it in the summer. 'Sustainability was an important consideration for me,' Ohm says. 'We used reclaimed Monterrey cypress for flooring and cabinetry, and the kitchen counters are from a company in Colorado that uses recycled composite materials. I used ipê for the decking, which is very durable.'

The interior is largely open-plan, and the study and bedroom connect freely with the sitting room, dining area and kitchen; only the bathroom is fully partitioned. The indoor-outdoor relationship is accentuated throughout, with three separate decks pointing to views in different directions. For Ohm, the quality of the relationship with the landscape itself is a key part of the cabin's success: 'I'm at just under 915 metres (3,000 feet), so not that high, but I'm at the top of the Mayacamas Mountains, so in the distance I can see Clear Lake, which is the second largest lake in California. I'm a few miles from the border of the Mendocino National Forest, and the land here is maintained by the state as a natural environment, so it's very much about living in nature. Each view has its own personality, and varies according to the time of day and the season.'

Hidden in a Desert Canyon

-

Olson Kundig: Sawmill,
Tehachapi, California, USA

Opposite, above and overleaf The wheel to one side of the central living area retracts the wall of glass at the front of the house, connecting inside and outside directly.

The mountains and high desert canyons of Tehachapi offer beautiful extremes and splendid isolation. The summers are hot and the winters decidedly cold, with snow on the hills and peaks, and the region is sparsely populated, with little in the way of infrastructure and services away from settlements and highways. A parcel of land on a former ranch offered Bruce Shafer and his family the opportunity to create a true escape.

'We wanted a retreat from city life and also a place for our family and friends to gather,' says Shafer, an engineer by training and now a senior executive in a construction materials company. 'We needed a place that could stand up to the extremes of the weather here, and a place where the ideas of "inside" and "outside" didn't need to have traditional boundaries. The beauty of this property reveals itself in its profound solitude and the expansive vistas.'

Down a long dirt track Shafer and his wife, Carol Horst, an artist and teacher, discovered a 14.5-hectare (36-acre) parcel of land in Sawmill Canyon that formed part of a larger ranch dating back to the late nineteenth century. There was once a sawmill not far away, along with former farm buildings, and a legacy herd of wild Morgan horses also inhabits the landscape. As well as ranching, the environment here has been affected by logging and mining, lending it something of a fragile quality. Shafer and his architect, Tom Kundig, were keen to adopt a light touch that would not only respect the surroundings but also encourage the slow healing process. 'The family wanted the house to give back to the land rather than take from it,' says Kundig. 'The sustainability and low-impact

environmental strategies were part of the original brief, and the biggest challenge was to minimize the building's impact while at the same time making it comfortable for family living.'

Given the natural conditions and seasonal variations, materials had to be hard-wearing and low-maintenance. Shafer, who also served as general contractor for the project, and Kundig settled on a structural framework of recycled steel in combination with precast concrete blocks. Much of the internal joinery is also recycled, taken from an old ranch barn, and the wheel that operates the sliding wall of glass at the front of the house is another found object.

The plan features a central living area, complete with a bespoke fireplace designed by Kundig and Shafer, with an integrated heat-recovery system. Three wings hold bedrooms and studio space for the couple and their two grown-up children, and there is also a choice of partially sheltered terraces protected by the overhanging roof, which – in combination with natural cross-ventilation and high-performance insulation – helps the house to stay cool in summer.

The property is entirely off-grid and self-sustaining. The house runs on solar power with battery storage, and has its own well; waste water is treated on the site and then used irrigate the land around the building. 'We wanted to explore how to make this house self-sufficient, durable and economical while also being comfortable,' says Kundig. 'I wanted to create an unpretentious, modern home that reflects the area's history and ecology, but one that weaves into its setting rather than stands apart from it.'

'We needed a place that could stand up to the extremes of the weather here and a place where the idea of "inside" and "outside" didn't need to have traditional boundaries.'

Previous pages, above and right The interiors are modern rustic in character: practical, hard-wearing and elegant. The joinery in the kitchen and elsewhere uses reclaimed timber found on the site.

Opposite The sliding glass wall at the front of the cabin floats to one side of the long terrace.

Sleeping Under the Stars

-

Waind Gohil + Potter Architects: SkyHut, various locations, Wales, UK

The SkyHut is a hybrid of cabin and caravan, with retractable doors and a folding roof that open the retreat to both land and sky.

One of the legends that surround the mountain of Cadair Idris suggests that anyone who sleeps on its slopes under the stars will wake up as either a madman or a poet. Some believe this legend is linked to an old tradition whereby poets and bards would camp out on the mountain seeking inspiration for their work. Such ideas have informed the evolution of the SkyHut, an off-grid cabin whose unfolding roof turns it into an observatory for gazing at the stars.

'The SkyHut is designed to provide a unique place to experience the Welsh sky, with doors and roof that open fully to transform the hut into a glamping observatory,' says the architect Phil Waind of Waind Gohil + Potter (WG+P) Architects. 'The idea of a retractable roof is particularly relevant to Wales, the country with the highest percentage of "international dark sky".'

The building is part of a project run by the glamping company Epic Retreats to develop a series of self-contained and self-sufficient cabins that can be easily transported to various rural locations in Wales, such as Snowdonia and the Llŷn Peninsula. WG+P has created a kinetic hut, capable not only of being transported but also of folding and unfolding, with solar-powered 'actuators' to crack the roof at will.

'The SkyHut is highly engineered, as it's no easy task to design a space that is transformable, transportable and off-grid,' says Waind. 'We had to ensure that the actuators could take the weight

of the roof and that the roof panels did not bend or twist when being opened. At the same time, we had to ensure that the interior would be totally weathertight when the roof was closed.'

The building itself is clad in corrugated metal panels that echo the simple outline and materiality of local farm buildings. A line of high clerestory windows between the panels and the roof suggests a modern twist and introduces light, while also accentuating the roof itself. Birch-faced plywood was used for the interior joinery, which includes a bed, cupboards and other simple facilities.

The SkyHut is fully insulated and off-grid, with two roof-mounted solar panels for electricity and warmth generated by a wood-burning stove; there is also a composting toilet and a sink. Water is stored in a separate container, brought to the site, while additional communal facilities on a campsite model – such as barbecues – can be provided when the cabin is used in combination with other retreats.

A hybrid home somewhere between permanence and the tent, the SkyHut offers a way of connecting with the natural surroundings and the night sky. 'We wanted to create a space that was functional and catered to the needs of its inhabitants,' says Waind. 'But we also wanted their stay to be fun and provide a unique experience. We have given the user the opportunity to transform the space at the flick of a switch and, being off-grid and transportable, that unique experience could be anywhere.'

Waterside
and Coast

Building a home in a remote and fragile place brings a particular sense of responsibility. Such projects involve a careful balancing act between protecting the place you love and creating a sheltered and inviting space in which to enjoy, understand and appreciate the surroundings. Immersion in nature and the natural world implies some kind of impact on the environment, yet the covenant of responsible homemaking suggests that we do all we can to reduce and mitigate that impact. Such responsibility becomes even more acute on coasts and shores, especially in isolated places and islands where nature holds sway and footprints of any kind stand out vividly.

Advances in building technology and micropower generation have created a tangible temptation to build homes and retreats in extreme settings and fragile environments that deserve protection as well as appreciation. Such settings demand not just respect but also great sensitivity, and the design of these buildings must be carried out in such a way that reduces their physical and carbon footprint.

The natural beauty and fragile ecology of places such as Fogo Island in Canada (see page 230) and Bruny Island off the coast of Tasmania (see page 224) rule out the idea of running electrical cables across the landscape or digging into the ground to lay miles of piping for water and mains services. In that respect, off-grid living has great advantages and provides practical solutions. Renewable sources of home-generated energy such as solar panels, wood-burning stoves and ground-source heat pumps create new opportunities for independent, year-round living while limiting environmental impact.

Yet in the context of remote islands or other extreme locations in places such as Canada, Scandinavia, Australia or New Zealand, solving the puzzle of providing energy and water is just one of a complex series of challenges, each of which has an environmental dimension. On a practical level, the lack of infrastructure and difficulties of access can create severe limitations when it comes to bringing in materials and labour, while long, hard winters can limit the available time for construction. Many of the projects in the following pages are accessible only by boat or helicopter, creating serious logistical problems.

In some cases, prefabrication has offered a solution. The Australian architectural practice Lai Cheong Brown used a combination of modular, factory-built units to construct the French Island Farmhouse (see page 206); the units were brought one at a time on a small car ferry across the waters of Western Port Bay, Victoria. Prefabrication helps to reduce time and labour on the site itself, which is especially helpful in remote settings, while reducing the overall carbon footprint by requiring less transportation than traditional piecemeal construction. The carbon footprint decreases, of course, when the modules are made from green materials such as sustainable timber. What is more, standards of insulation are generally higher in factory-made modules, reducing the energy consumption of the building once it is up and running.

In the United Kingdom, the prefabrication specialist Boutique Modern created a tailored modular home for a waterside setting in Dorset (see page 178). The factory-built units that form Buck's Coppice were delivered by truck down narrow country lanes and swung into place, while a combination of solar panels and other on-site resources allows the house to function as an off-grid retreat. Prefabrication techniques have been used to great effect in other remote settings, such as for the Clear Lake It House in the Californian mountains near Mendocino National Forest (see previous chapter, page 154).

Logistical challenges combined with the desire to build in a sustainable, low-carbon manner have helped to dictate the choice of materials used to construct the homes in these pages. Imported materials tend to be light and easily transportable, as seen in Todd Saunders's Bridge Studio on Fogo Island (see page 230), where they had to be brought in by boat and/or carried by hand. Similar considerations applied to many other island projects, including Mary Arnold-Forster's Scotasay House in the Western Isles of Scotland, where everything and everyone involved in the project had to come in by boat.

The architect Adam Thom decided to treat his own Canadian island retreat as a summerhouse that would be shut up over the winter months. This allowed him to build Molly's Cabin near Pointe au Baril (see page 174) with a lighter palette of materials – principally local and reclaimed timber – but even so every piece had to come across the water, working to a tight seasonal schedule that allowed no construction during the long winter.

In such settings localism makes more sense than ever, since it reduces the challenges of transportation and cuts down on fuel miles. In almost every instance on these pages, materials have been locally and responsibly sourced, with an emphasis on sustainably farmed timber. In some cases, as with Molly's Cabin, reclaimed and recycled materials are put to good use; Thom obtained much of his wood from old barns nearby.

In another project on Bruny Island in Tasmania, the architect John Wardle employed a palette of organic materials for the construction of the Shearers' Quarters (see page 242), including internal panelling made from timber boxes that had once been used to store apples. For the design and construction of his own waterside summerhouse at Lundnäs (see page 188), the Swedish architect Buster Delin was able to salvage and reuse stone and brick from a factory that had once stood on the site, and he found other materials locally and regionally.

It is also encouraging to hear such architects – and their clients – talking not only of respecting the landscape around them, while treading as lightly as possible on it, but also of helping the environment. Wardle, for instance, has engaged in an extensive conservation programme on his farmstead on Bruny Island, encouraging reforestation and the revival of the natural habitat.

Similarly, the owners of the exhausted former farmland on which the Eyrie Cabins (see page 200) are set, designed by Cheshire Architects on New Zealand's North Island, have been engaged with a project to replant trees and shrubs while encouraging wildlife to return. Such examples could be seen as a way of offsetting any impact to the environment caused by the process of construction, and in effect such off-grid residents take on the role of environmental guardians.

The Edge of the Archipelago

-

Agathom Co.: Molly's Cabin,
Pointe au Baril, Ontario, Canada

The architect owners describe the house, with its wraparound roof, as a 'wooden tent', a simple but effective summer shelter.

A crucial consideration in the evolution of an off-grid home is how and when it will be used. A case in point is Molly's Cabin, on a remote island on the eastern edge of Georgian Bay. The winters are extreme, and few inhabitants choose to spend the coldest months there, although in the summer the population swells and the summer cottages open their doors. From the start, then, the architects and owners of Molly's Cabin decided that this off-grid house would be used for only three seasons of the year at most. Even so, the project presented many challenges.

'The cabin is on the outer edge of an elaborate and extensive archipelago where the islands are made of igneous granite, scraped and sculpted by glaciers,' says Adam Thom of Agathom Co., the architectural practice he founded in Toronto with his Danish wife, Katja. 'Building on an island without electricity that is 13 kilometres (8 miles) from the nearest marina is a challenge, and the building season is short. It's absolutely impossible to work here during the winter, from the freeze right up to the spring thaw.'

The Thoms decided to design and build a modestly scaled, contextual home without the services and facilities that might be needed for year-round residence. Molly's Cabin, which they describe as a 'wooden tent', has a distinctive wraparound shingle roof enclosing a timber building that splices vernacular and modernist influences.

The single-storey cabin sits on granite boulders close to the water's edge, with a backdrop of trees. Since all the building materials had to come in by boat, the Thoms kept the palette simple. The timber framework and much of the other joinery consist of reclaimed and recycled pine taken from former Ontario barns; many of the beams are hundreds of years old. The cladding is cedar and the roof is asphalt.

An open-plan dining area and kitchen leads out to a substantial deck, and there is also a sitting room, a library and a bedroom. The principal source of heat is a central fireplace, complemented by a stove in the kitchen. An array of solar panels provides electricity for lighting, refrigeration and the pump that draws water from the lake; a composting toilet is in an outhouse nearby.

'We are impressed by how the building keeps giving,' says Adam. 'It's really pleasing to see the cottage in full use by the whole family – children, parents, grandparents. We wanted the design to create many routes to the exterior, and while the rock landscape is rugged it is also a delicate ecosystem. Despite the pressure of climate change, development and pollution, the region is home to a vast and gorgeous spectrum of animals, many of which are endangered. The project fits our tradition of responding fully to the site, which is a constant theme in our work.'

Opposite The principal source of heat is the central fireplace with its stone surround, which is used on colder evenings; the open-plan nature of the living spaces allows warmth to circulate freely.

Below Banks of floor-to-ceiling glass in the living area frame views of the water and the archipelago, and the surrounding granite shelf forms a natural terrace.

Between the Woods and the Lake

-

Boutique Modern: Buck's Coppice,
Hooke, Dorset, UK

The cabin is anchored to the shore but has a deck that cantilevers over the water, creating the impression that the house is floating.

179

'The house fits perfectly into the woodland and the lakeside setting. We thought carefully about the position and size of every window and have views where we want them, as well as morning and evening light. It really is a beautiful spot.'

For many years the carpenter Sid Allen spent time living in a caravan on a picturesque plot of land in Dorset, near where he grew up. The setting is rural and remote, overlooking one of the small lakes that punctuate the hinterlands around the River Hooke, south of Yeovil. Eventually Allen and his partner, Sandra Whipham, a documentary film producer, managed to buy the land and began thinking about how they could create a holiday and weekend home that would suit the setting and – in the absence of any utility services – be fully off-grid.

'It's very isolated and a Site of Special Scientific Interest,' says Allen. 'Connecting a new building to mains water or electricity was financially prohibitive and completely impractical, as there's no available infrastructure nearby. So I began looking into alternatives.'

For the building itself, Allen needed something that would comply with planning restrictions on the site, which allowed only a structure that was classed as a mobile home. He settled on a prefabricated home designed and built by the English company Boutique Modern, which not only complies with such requirements but also could be delivered in modules on trucks that could navigate the narrow lanes characteristic of this part of the world. Working closely with the company, Allen and Whipham – who have a young child – were able to tailor the design to meet their needs and that of the lakeside setting.

'The building had to be constructed so that it could sit on driven piles by the lake, and we wanted to focus everything on the water and make the most of the view,' says Allen. 'The house was put in place by crane on the banks of the lake, and I constructed a large deck over the water itself so that we could walk directly out on to it from the house.'

Facing up to the challenge of providing warmth, water and power, Allen came up with a collection of off-grid solutions. Water comes from the lake itself, filtered for use, while waste water is treated with a Biorock treatment system and returned to the land. A wood-burning stove is the main source of heat, helped by high levels of insulation within the structure of the factory-built house. Photovoltaic panels provide electricity in combination with battery storage, and bottled gas is used for the cooking range. A back-up generator kicks in only if other systems fail, while the services are housed in a small structure close to the main building.

'The house fits perfectly into the woodland and the lakeside setting,' says Allen, who completed the interiors himself. 'We thought carefully about the position and size of every window and have views where we want them, as well as morning and evening light. It really is a beautiful spot.'

Above Glazing frames views over the quiet water, as here in the bedroom.

Left The kitchen island and the rest of the interior joinery were crafted and completed by the cabin's owner, Sid Allen.

A Refuge in the Wilderness

-

Apio Arquitectos: Casa Todos los Santos,
Lago Todos los Santos, Patagonia, Chile

Left The cabin's elevated position on the hillside
makes it a dramatic vantage point, looking over
the lake to the mountains beyond.

Opposite and pages 186–87 The house sits on
a steel platform anchored to the steep slope, with
a walkway that ascends from the dock below.

Waterside and Coast

This page and opposite Bedrooms are pushed to each end of the house and service spaces are at the back. The living spaces at the centre are partially open-plan, with a short wall and internal window sectioning off the kitchen.

The journey to Patricia Chadwick and Christian Rodriguez's lakeside refuge in southern Chile involves a plane ride, a car journey, a boat trip and a walk. With three children to consider, it is not the easiest of commutes to a home designed and built principally for weekends and holidays. But they try to spend as much time at the house as they possibly can, because the rewards are many in a place immersed in an astonishing landscape and well beyond the reach of phone signals and internet connections.

The cabin sits on a hillside on the edge of Lago Todos los Santos, in an area of national parks and protected reserves. It is a cinematic setting, looking across the waters of the lake to the Andes mountains beyond and two volcanoes, Osorno and Puntiagudo. 'We love the fact that the house has been inserted into the mountainside and has become part of it,' says Chadwick. 'It's a simple house, but it has everything you could need and it's warm in winter and fresh in the summer. It's all you need for a simple life, and yet it captures the natural environment and has the most stunning views.'

The family turned to the architect Angie Chadwick Stuardo (who happens to be Patricia's sister) of Apio Arquitectos to design the house. The remote setting in combination with the gradient of the hillside and the complete lack of any grid-based services or infrastructure created a series of challenges that had to be addressed creatively. 'After living through the process of constructing this house, I think we could manage a project almost anywhere,' says

Stuardo. 'We wanted to design a simple, low-maintenance house while causing the least impact on the environment. Our goal is that the architecture belongs to the natural setting so that the setting becomes the protagonist. For me, the house is a refuge on the cliff where you can admire nature and become part of it.'

Stuardo designed a steel-framed platform that floats on the hillside and creates a strong, stable base for the house, which was constructed with a timber frame coated in hard-wearing metallic wall and roof plates. This choice of materials means the cabin is well able to withstand the extremes of the climate and potential seismic shifts. A central living space opens up to views of the lake and flows out on to a substantial elevated veranda and deck. Two bedrooms are at either end of the house, and service spaces are at the rear.

At present, the main source of electrical power is an independent generator. Given the weather conditions and site of the house, with limited sunshine hours and copious tree cover, the installation of solar panels will depend on the availability of an extremely efficient system. Water comes from the mountainside and is held in storage tanks, and waste water is treated on the site; any refuse must be removed by boat. 'It is all about nature and its conservation,' says Chadwick. 'The house is in a protected national park, far from "civilization". It is a magical and unique place.'

Tranquility by
the River

-

Delin Arkitektkontor: Lundnäs House,
Arbrå, Sweden

The summerhouse offers a picture frame for
viewing the river, but also provides a sense of
intimate connection with the woodland in
which it sits.

Above Private spaces, namely the two bedrooms and the bathroom, are at the rear, while the galley kitchen is to one side of the corridor that connects all parts of the house.

Right A curving wall containing the hearth separates the open-plan living area from the rest of the house.

Opposite Sheets of floor-to-ceiling glass connect the seating area to the emerald greenery and treescape outside.

The Swedish architect Buster Delin's summerhouse evolved over the course of seven years, an experimental case-study project that is 'completely synchronized with nature'. Both designed and built by him, it served as a way to explore his own ideas about sustainability, including using repurposed and locally available materials.

'The biggest challenge was to carry through the project as both architect and client,' says Delin, whose practice is based in Stockholm. 'The solution was to build slowly and allow the design and construction to develop simultaneously, thus giving my ideas time to mature. This is also the strength of the project. It created a result that is well thought through.'

The house sits by the water's edge in an area defined by its combination of countless lakes and verdant forest, about three hours' drive north of Stockholm. The environmental sensitivity of the location and the beauty of the surroundings were important considerations from the start, and the architect's aim was to craft a rounded response to this tranquil and delightful setting.

The riverfront site itself was once home to a factory that produced ceramic stoves, and traces of this industrial heritage remained. Delin was able to reuse the foundations of the factory as a solid plinth to support the new house, while also recycling stone and brick, which form the more enclosed portion of the house. Other materials, such as the timber for the roof and linen for the curtains, were acquired locally.

The rest of the house is best described as a glass pavilion, facing the water, with floor-to-ceiling windows offering constant interaction with the landscape and the river. This part of the building, which connects with a terrace to the front, holds an open-plan living space, including seating and dining areas. An important part of the whole is a curving wall that forms a backdrop to this multifunctional space and contains a fireplace, a wood store and – to the rear – a small galley kitchen. The more enclosed section of the house contains two bedrooms and a compact shower room plus a composting toilet.

The fireplace is the only source of heating, apart from solar gain, and the heat from the fire is diffused through the building via a layer of clay pellets under the concrete slab; this combination of clay and concrete retains warmth, as does the stone and brickwork. Water comes from the site, and waste water is filtered via a private treatment system. Local renewable energy supplies the small amount of power needed for lighting and other uses, although this is minimal given the summer-centric pattern of living. The entire house can be secured and the water system drained during the winter, when the temperature falls well below freezing.

Opposite and left The pavilion sits discreetly in the landscape, partially sheltered by its backdrop of trees, but is also orientated to make the most of river views.

Below The master bedroom at the back has walls of reclaimed stone, in contrast with the transparency of the main living spaces.

Reflections on the Lagoon

-

Mary Arnold-Forster: Scotasay House,
Isle of Harris, Scotland, UK

Opposite The bedroom pavilion offers framed glimpses of the rugged coast and tidal waters.

Above The cabin is split into two distinct parts, one for the living spaces and one for the bedrooms, with a substantial, partially sheltered deck between them looking out over the lagoon.

The architect Mary Arnold-Forster likes to call this off-grid island home the Golden Cabin. The name evokes the way the sunlight reflects off the water of the lagoon beside the house and illuminates its birch-clad façade. Yet it also suggests the special nature of the project for both architect and client, who overcame various challenges to design and build a home that would suit year-round living in a place with no utility services of any kind. The success of the house lay ultimately not only in the design of the building itself, but also in recent advances in small-scale energy generation, which make self-sufficiency possible and practical in situations such as this.

The island has been in the owner's family for many years, and was already home to an old croft house and a modest cabin. Gas canisters and drinking water had to be brought in for every stay, and ultimately the damp and cold made the buildings untenable during any but the warmest months. The owner turned to Arnold-Forster, formerly of Dualchas and now head of her own practice.

'He wanted a cabin like the one he experienced during his childhood, but one that was dry and warm, and that worked,' says Arnold-Forster. 'Materials had to be robust and the house needed to connect to the tidal lagoon. The owner is very attuned to the tide and the sea, and an expert boatman. We wanted to tread lightly on the land and cantilever over the lagoon.'

The single-storey, heavily insulated timber cabin was designed as a series of complementary pods, with a sheltered deck between the spaces devoted to living and sleeping. The butterfly roofs of these pods channel rainwater, which is harvested and stored for use in an underground tank. The main living space is warmed by a wood-burning stove, while electricity is provided by a combination of a wind turbine and solar power; the bedroom pods are heated by this self-generated electricity.

'The area is one of extreme natural beauty, with abundant wildlife, but totally off the grid, so we had no choice but to explore self-sufficiency,' says Arnold-Forster's client and friend, a businessman with a strong interest in architecture and design. 'It was both exciting and challenging. Living here, you become more aware of the energy you use, and balance its use according to the weather. We now have a combination of wind and solar power, so dull, windless days are not good for washing clothes or baking, but on bright, breezy days we can switch everything on and then a large bank of batteries stores energy you don't use, so at night you know the lights won't go out.' The house is now his full-time residence: 'I love the beautiful light, the views and the warm, dry, uncluttered design. It's a modern cabin in a special location of dreams and inspiration.'

'I love the beautiful light, the views and the warm, dry, uncluttered design. It's a modern cabin in a special location of dreams and inspiration.'

Opposite Service spaces, such as the kitchen, have been pushed to the rear, and are lit naturally through skylights and clerestory windows.

Above The deck is partly protected by the pavilions to either side, creating an enticing outdoor room where the eye is channelled towards the lagoon.

Right The spine corridor to the rear doubles as storage, with generous fitted bookshelves.

Opposite, above and below The two parts of the Golden Cabin establish a vivid and direct relationship with the water, and the constant motion of the tide offers subtle shifts and changes throughout the day.

Opposite and below The living space is open-plan, with zones for seating and dining; the kitchen is behind the dining area.

Complementary Coastal Cabins

-

Cheshire Architects: Eyrie Cabins,
Kaipara, North Island, New Zealand

Left Clad in charred cedar, the twin cabins
sit unencumbered in the open landscape,
their sculptural forms like works of land art.

Opposite The ground floor of each cabin is
devoted to an open-plan living space, with a
fitted kitchenette to one side; picture windows
frame views of the coast.

The coastal landscape in this part of Kaipara, on the northern tip of New Zealand's North Island, has a rugged character beyond the postcard picturesque. The land has been exhausted by farming, while the shore, not far from Kaipara Harbour, consists of tidal inlets rich in mangrove. Two friends, a gallerist and a biologist, bought a plot of former farmland with the intention of restoring the landscape through replanting and encouraging the revival of local wildlife.

At first the two friends camped out on the site in little more than a shed. Planning codes allowed the design and construction of a substantial home, but instead they commissioned two small, off-grid cabins from Nat Cheshire and Ian Scott of Cheshire Architects. Simple, crafted and abstract, the twin structures have the sculptural quality of land art, forming crisp, geometric shapes on a green hillside overlooking the coast.

'The Eyrie Cabins have an organic minimalism and modest splendour,' says Cheshire. 'Something about the tiny scale of the houses afforded us this opportunity for unprecedented precision, concision and resolution. It almost felt like making cabinetry rather than houses.'

Set some distance apart to afford the two friends a degree of privacy, and focused on differing views of the landscape, the cabins are clad in charred cedar, reinforcing the sense of abstraction against the verdant green of the hill. The lower level of each structure contains an open-plan living space with a galley kitchen to one side and a toilet tucked discreetly under the stairs that climb to a mezzanine sleeping platform.

There are, however, subtle differences between the two interiors. One of the cabins features internal joinery and panelling in plywood, while the other uses black formply that is so dark 'that it's like living in a drop of ink', as Cheshire puts it. Both cabins, with these contrasting light and dark interiors, have brass kitchen niches like a piece of crafted jewellery within a storage wall.

The cabins are entirely autonomous, creating an experience reminiscent of the first camping expeditions to the property. Electricity is provided by solar panels, while rainwater harvesting provides water. Each cabin has an outdoor shower, and the water used, along with treated septic waste, is returned to the soil to support the replanting programme.

In some ways, the houses are reminiscent of vernacular New Zealand bachs, the region's simple wooden beach houses, yet they possess an artistry that sets them apart. 'We wanted forms in the land that would refuse to resolve into the shorthand of a "house",' says Cheshire. 'They had to pair the extraordinary with the organic.'

Opposite The two cabins sit gently in natural tucks and folds in the topography, while the surrounding land has been revived with fresh indigenous planting.

This page The crafted interiors have a strong sense of organic warmth and a number of fitted, integrated elements, such as niches for the kitchenettes. For contrast, one of the interiors is fitted in plywood and the other in inky-black formply.

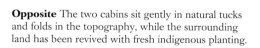

Waterside and Coast

Below At night the cabins glow like lanterns in the darkness, forming subtle beacons on the coast.

Opposite The large picture windows of each structure frame views of both land and sea, exploring the relationship between the two, while offering privacy from the neighbouring cabin.

Tranquil Island Living

\-

Lai Cheong Brown: French Island Farmhouse,
French Island, Western Port Bay, Victoria, Australia

Opposite, above and pages 210–11 Sitting
discreetly in the landscape, the linear, low-lying
house is formed from a collection of prefabricated
modules brought to the island by ferry.

At the heart of Western Port Bay, about 65 kilometres (40 miles) southeast of Melbourne, French Island is home to a large national park and just over 100 residents. There are no mains utility services of any kind on the island itself, which is managed by a community association. Unlike its neighbour, Phillip Island, French Island has no bridge to the mainland, so everyone and everything comes across by passenger ferry or a small car ferry. While the isolation and unspoilt beauty of the island are alluring, building a home there presents a raft of challenges, as the architect Rowan Brown soon discovered when his parents, Ken and Helen Brown, commissioned a farmhouse.

'For this project, sustainability was not an ethical or even intellectual position but a practical necessity, because there was simply no option other than a self-sustaining house,' says Brown, whose practice is based in Melbourne. 'It had to be self-sustaining in terms of power, water and waste, and affordability also had to be addressed, since building in such a remote place can have a significant impact on building costs. Also, the house had to be able to accommodate more than its two usual residents at short notice, because the weather often leads to visitors being marooned.'

Given these constraints, Lai Cheong Brown began looking at prefabrication as a potential solution. The practice developed the idea of a modular home, keeping in mind that each module must fit on to the car ferry. In addition, the structural framework of the house, along with the choice of materials to build it, had to be robust enough to withstand the winds that come in from the Bass Strait and the corrosive nature of the salt spray on a site not far from the shore.

Rather than taking inspiration from vernacular farmhouses, which are typically rectangular structures with verandas, the architect and clients chose a courtyard formation that would provide a sheltered outdoor space protected from the breeze. The heavily insulated, modular living spaces are arranged around this outdoor room, with bedrooms in the wings to either side and service spaces around a walkway and entrance zone, while an open-plan arrangement of seating and dining spaces plus the kitchen inhabits the fourth section of the house. A separate building, or outrigger, holds much of the kit needed to sustain the house, along with back-up systems, including a generator.

The main source of heating is a wood-fired stove, and the cooking range is also fuelled by timber. Electricity comes from photovoltaic panels, while hot water is provided via solar tubes. Rainwater is harvested and stored in two tanks, one of which provides a potable supply for the house and the other an emergency store for fighting bush fires. All waste must be handled on the site; a worm-farm septic system deals with grey waste and will in future provide irrigation for a small citrus orchard that the owners hope to establish nearby.

Opposite and left The living spaces are arranged around a central courtyard, which serves as a secondary circulation space and introduces light and air to all parts of the house.

Below The courtyard is also a vital outdoor room, a sheltered, multifunctional open-air space protected from the sea breezes that are common to the island.

Channelling the Breeze

-

Modersohn & Freiesleben: Roth House,
Queenstown, New Brunswick, Canada

Accordion glass doors on either side of the building unfold to create a breezeway at the heart of the house, which sits on a bluff overlooking the lake.

The Roth House in rural New Brunswick is an exemplar of contextual design with just a few small exceptions. The architect, Modersohn & Freiesleben, is based in Berlin, and shipped the long run of accordion doors that sits to either side of the building's central living space from Germany. Yet everything else is about localism, both in the design of the house itself and in the choice of materials.

'The clients wanted a simple wooden house, with a strong connection to the familiar, vernacular farm buildings of the West Coast, and concurrently modern,' says the architect, Antje Freiesleben, who met the Roth family when they were living in Berlin. 'Residential buildings in a rural setting have been one of our recurring tasks. Whether they are in Germany or Canada, our houses always pick up on shapes, types and materials from the local building tradition, which we interpret in a contemporary way.'

The house is on a plot of land that had belonged to the family for many years, and was commissioned by the art historian Harriet Roth and her late husband, Martin Roth, former director of the Victoria and Albert Museum in London, as a holiday home for themselves and their grown-up children. It is set on a gentle green ridge overlooking Otnabog Lake, which sits alongside the St John River; the city of the same name is to the south.

'The house had to fit into the style of the area and be habitable for two adults most of the time and our children on

and off,' says Harriet. 'We wanted to be able to work in peace and quiet surrounded by nature, with views across the lake and light and sun throughout the house.'

Influenced by local barns and farm buildings, the two-storey house is made from timber, with sheltered porches and a steeply pitched roof. The glazed central section of the lower storey opens up to either side to create a breezeway that passes right through the heart of the building, helping to cool the house in the summer. At other times the principal source of heating is a wood-burning stove in the living room, which is at one end of the house; the kitchen and family room are at the other. Upstairs are three bedrooms and a bathroom.

The wood to build the house was all found locally. Black spruce was used for the cladding, red pine for the floors, white cedar for the porches and white pine from the property itself for trim and detailing. The roof is of metal sheeting, reminiscent of farmsteads.

The house has its own well and waste-water treatment system. Electrical power for lighting currently comes from local renewable sources, principally wind power, but there is a medium-term plan to install a photovoltaic array on the south-facing side of the roof to achieve greater self-sufficiency.

Waterside and Coast

Previous pages and opposite There are porches at either end of the house, which also has a slim veranda on each side.

Below A timber staircase at the centre of the house, alongside the dining area, was designed and built with a light touch so that it does not impose itself on the space.

Embracing the Seasons

–

Omas:Works: Land House,
Meaford, Ontario, Canada

The L-shaped house is sensitively sited in a gap
in the trees, looking down over the lake.

Above A porch by the main entrance doubles as a wood store; the separate sauna also has a mini breezeway.

Right and opposite The living spaces are to one side of the breezeway, and the bedrooms to the other; wood-burning stoves are the principal source of heat.

Dogtrot houses are defined by their central breezeways, which form a partially sheltered space at the heart of the building, under the roof but open to the landscape at either side. They are more commonly seen in the southern states of America, where the breezeway helps to cool the house, positioned between a simple living room and kitchen on one side and a bedroom or two on the other. They are not so common in the colder climate of Canada, but Joel and Michelle Loblaw (a landscape and furniture designer respectively) insisted on such a plan for the design of their home in Meaford, Ontario, not far from the shore of Nottawasaga Bay.

'The effect of the dogtrot here is that the owners are constantly forced to engage with the environment, the weather and the landscape as they pass from one part of the house to the other,' says the designer Brian O'Brian of Omas:Works. 'I have been fascinated by dogtrots for years, so the opportunity to build one was very welcome. Beyond that, the key ideas here relate to the sense of being held within a volume while simultaneously being reminded of where you are and your connections to the land.'

The Loblaws bought the property some years ago, and initially camped on the site beside the substantial pond before self-building a simple off-grid 'bunkie', or sleeping cabin. Eventually they decided to commission a new house on the property, which they call 'the Land', to serve as a holiday and weekend home for themselves and their two young children. 'We've been coming up to the Land for years, and we have raised our kids with this as part of their lives,' they say. 'Brian knew we wanted to live in a way where we would be part of the landscape, and that we wanted to feel truly at home every time we arrive here.'

The single-storey house was designed and built to a modest budget, keeping the environmental sensitivity of the Land – which is in a conservation area – in mind throughout, along with the need for a low-maintenance and hard-wearing retreat. It is clad in tongue-and-groove cedar siding, and roofed with sheets of agricultural steel. Inside, the principal material for walls and ceilings is untreated plywood, and the floors are timber. The living room and kitchen sit at one end of the house, and there are three bedrooms across the breezeway. Joel has also created a series of outdoor rooms, plus a sauna, including a fully functioning outdoor kitchen with wood-fired oven.

Heating is provided by two wood-burning stoves, one in the living room and a second in the master bedroom (there is a third in the old bunkie), while natural cross ventilation is assisted in the summer by the dogtrot plan and opening windows to either side. Water comes from a well on the site, and the house has its own septic treatment system. The house is largely self-sufficient, although there is modest electrical provision from the grid, which is principally and sparingly used for lighting during winter visits.

Waterside and Coast

Right The bedrooms are designed and finished simply, using plywood for the walls and ceilings in combination with timber floors.

Below The sauna is in a separate small building by the lake, in a similar style to the main house.

Opposite The central breezeway not only draws in fresh air, but also offers a sheltered outdoor room – a hybrid of porch and veranda.

A Home at the Ends of the Earth

-

Room II: D'Entrecasteaux House,
Bruny Island, Tasmania, Australia

The house is anchored by its stone walls, which also enclose the internal living spaces and shelter outdoor rooms such as the courtyard.

'We wanted to create a sense of resonance with the geological ensemble of the Tasmanian landscape and to set up a relationship with the place itself.'

As you arrive on Bruny Island after a ferry crossing from the small Tasmanian town of Kettering, the tourist literature tells you to 'relax, you're on Bruny Time'. There is certainly a more sedate pace and a very different quality of life on Bruny, which feels like the end of the earth – but in the most positive way. The island landscape is mesmerizing, dominated by a combination of farmland and national park. Bruny is particularly important for its bird colonies, and is home to the world's largest population of endangered pardalote, along with short-tailed shearwater and swift parrots.

In this extraordinary place to make a home, rich in challenges but also in rewards, the architectural practice Room 11 has created a sculptural, low-slung net zero residence named after the D'Entrecasteaux Channel, which separates Bruny from the mainland. Both channel and island were named after the French naval officer Bruni d'Entrecasteaux, who explored the region in the 1790s.

'We were interested in creating a sense of psychological security in a remote setting,' says Thomas Bailey of Room 11, a practice with offices in both Hobart and Melbourne. 'We wanted to create a sense of resonance with the geological ensemble of the Tasmanian landscape and to set up a relationship with the place itself.'

The building sits low in the landscape, embedded into a gentle hill with views out across the shore. Stone walls protect the house and also enclose a sheltered courtyard by the main entrance; a more open deck is at the front of the building. The internal footprint is very modest, with an open-plan living area and kitchen at its heart, plus a master suite and an additional compact bedroom. The modest scale, in combination with high levels of insulation, helps to reduce the overall energy needs of the house.

Rainwater is collected and stored for use in four large steel tanks; waste water is treated on the site and returned to the soil. Energy is provided by a solar array, and the excess is sold back to the grid via a cable link; at times of peak demand, power can be drawn back to the house from the local network, which is principally supported by hydroelectricity. A Tesla home battery is due to be installed, so that more energy from the solar panels can be stored at the house. Passive strategies are also employed, and the house benefits from solar gain during the winter and natural ventilation in the warmer months. 'The sustainability value also lies in the specification of robust materials and simple, logical principles,' says Bailey. 'The house is very modest, but it also has solidity and permanence.'

Opposite The house offers framed views of the D'Entrecasteaux Channel, with the Tasmanian 'mainland' in the distance.

Right The stone walls give this modest, low-slung house a degree of permanence and even monumentality, in the manner of a fortress.

Below and overleaf A wide timber deck at the front of the house faces the coast; the enclosed courtyard offers a more sheltered outdoor room.

Apostrophes in
the Landscape

-

Saunders Architecture: Bridge Studio,
Deep Bay, Fogo Island, Newfoundland, Canada

Opposite, below and pages 234–35 The Bridge Studio is one of several small, sculptural artists' retreats on this sparsely populated island.

Right The building is orientated towards
the view across an inland pool, and accessed
over a bridge to the rear.

Opposite Compact, ordered and modest,
the studio culminates in a fitted desk by the
picture window, offering a workstation with
an extraordinary prospect.

The ecology of remote and extreme places can often be summed up in the phrase 'fragile beauty'. These are places where flora and fauna work hard to survive, and where the ecosystem is finely balanced. Fogo Island, off the northeastern coast of Newfoundland, is a good example. The island was historically a base for fishermen, who pushed out into the open waters of the Atlantic in search of cod. Today it is best known for its artists' residency programme, supported by the Fogo Island Arts corporation, which is in turn funded by a foundation established by two entrepreneurs who grew up there.

An important element of the residency programme is the provision of six sculptural studios on different parts of the coast, designed by the architect Todd Saunders. Each was designed individually in response to the specific conditions of its site. But they do have elements in common: all are modest in scale, sensitive to the environment and self-sufficient. They play with ideas of elevation in various ways, providing lookout posts facing the water, while splicing contemporary sculptural forms with inspiration from vernacular fishermen's huts and storage sheds. Together, they form a family of buildings that share a common language.

'The studios are like apostrophes on the landscape, and they can be viewed either from a distance or close up and from many different angles, so it was really important that they weren't all the same,' says Saunders. 'There are a lot of hiking trails on the island, and as you walk past the studios they seem to change in form and shape. They are extremely sculptural.'

Given the remote nature of the site, as well as of the island itself, the studios had to be fully off the grid; most are designed for daytime use, but sometimes in some of the six studios (where there's enough space) artists have the option of staying the night. The building materials had to be light enough to be transported by hand, while the specification of insulation and glazing had to be high. Most of the studios are raised above the ground on piloti, not just to accentuate the views but also to avoid disturbing the plant life and lichens.

The Bridge Studio is in Deep Bay, in the west of the island. Projecting from a ridge that overlooks an inland pool, the studio forms a floating platform suspended in the landscape, with a compact, crafted living space culminating in a fitted desk before a picture window that overlooks the water. The studio is warmed by a wood-burning stove, and power is provided by a solar array nearby. The studio is paired with a restored saltbox house nearby that provides a composting toilet, fed by harvested rainwater.

All six studios are fully autonomous, as Saunders explains: 'The whole idea was that these were such pristine sites that you couldn't start digging into the ground for sewage pipes or dragging electricity lines out to them, which would be absurd. They feel new every time I visit, depending on the weather, the seasons, and who I am experiencing them with socially. When I am there in person they feel almost mystical.'

Past and Present

-

Stinessen Arkitektur: Josefvatnet Cabin,
Josefvatnet, Troms, Norway

Opposite The old cabin and the new sit side by side in a clearing overlooking the lake.

Below The living area offers a panorama of the lake, but also looks out on to a deck, which forms an outdoor room at one end of the house.

Right and overleaf The open deck is connected to a more sheltered porch, which also protects the main entrance.

Below and opposite Wood-burning stoves heat the bedrooms, which offer vivid connections with the outdoors through picture windows.

A cabin and a cottage on a hillside overlooking Lake Josefvatnet in northern Norway offer a telling contrast between old and new. Bjørn Viggo Ottem and Marit Stagrum Ottem have owned both properties for many years, including a historic timber cabin dating from the eighteenth century and painted the traditional falu red that is common to the cottages, farmhouses and barns of the region. The cottage – itself totally off-grid – has a charm of its own, as well as a delightful position overlooking the lake, but it proved to be almost unusable beyond the summer months.

The Ottems, who have three children, asked the architect Snorre Stinessen to design an annexe that would be suited to year-round living, even in the freezing temperatures of the Arctic winter. Stinessen created a distinctly modern building alongside the old, although they share modesty of scale, an organic palette of materials and sensitivity to the environment.

'We decided that the annexe should be detached from the existing cabin to create a necessary and respectful space around it,' says Stinessen. 'The layout links the exit from the living room of the old cabin in a direct line with a covered gallery, or porch, that gives access to all the individual rooms of the new building. But in contrast, we wanted the annexe to play up to the natural setting and integrate the beautiful views.'

The new cabin combines picture windows with timber walls that are 50 centimetres (nearly 20 inches) thick and packed with insulation. The cladding is of local pine and the interior panelling and joinery knot-free alder. The thickness of the walls allows the insertion of integrated elements such as shelving and window seats. Given the remote location, some 100 kilometres (60 miles) south of Tromsø, all materials had to be brought in either by boat or by helicopter.

The main living space at one end of the house offers extensive views of the lake, while also overlooking a deck to one side. Off this space is a sleeping nook, and there is a small bedroom in the centre and a larger master bedroom at the far end of the cabin, connecting with a simple bathroom.

The principal sources of heating are two wood-burning stoves, one in the master bedroom and one in the living room, both fed with firewood from the local forest. Lighting is provided by a solar panel, while water comes from a well; there is a composting toilet, and grey water is also treated on the site.

Like the old, the new cabin is fully self-sufficient, but the sophistication of the design means that it can be used at any time of year. 'Our priorities were functionality for summer and winter use, being more or less maintenance-free, using natural materials and having this contrast between the modern building and the old cabin,' say the Ottems. 'What we enjoy most about the new cabin is the visual quality of the building, along with the way that it doesn't dominate the setting.'

Farmstead
by the Sea

-

John Wardle Architects: Shearers' Quarters,
Waterview, Bruny Island, Tasmania, Australia

Opposite The dining area is part of a spacious living space that also contains seating and the kitchen.

Above The new cabin is a sculptural form in the landscape, defined partly by the irregular geometry of its tin roof.

243

runy Island, off the coast of Tasmania, is the kind of place that stays in the memory. Some thirty years after a childhood trip to the island, the architect John Wardle found himself returning after spotting a farm for sale there. Waterview had failed at auction and was languishing on the market, but Wardle and his wife were captivated instantly.

The farmland itself was in poor condition and required thorough and patient restoration. It is now a productive farm once more, with between 1,500 and 2,000 head of fine-wool merino sheep and lambs. The 495-hectare (1,220-acre) farm includes pasture, arable land for livestock feed, a good deal of forest and a natural preserve.

The original farmhouse sits at the end of a dirt road that winds down through the property as the land falls away towards the sea. It was built in the 1840s on a promontory overlooking Storm Bay, creating a perfect vantage point for appreciating the coast and watching the sea traffic. 'Unusually, it was built by a mariner and not a farmer,' says Wardle. 'Captain Kelly placed it on the edge of a cliff so that he could see out over the ocean; a farmer would have built closer to the main road. Kelly was one of the fathers of Tasmania's whaling industry, and there was a historic whaling station on the property dating from 1820.'

Echoes and relics of former structures dot the landscape around the farmhouse. One of these was a sheep-shearing shed, which appears in grainy photographs taken in the 1940s, sitting near the farmhouse. The positioning of the old shed ties in closely with a dynamic new building that Wardle has built beside the farmhouse,

called the Shearers' Quarters, which accommodates family and friends as well as the seasonal shearers.

The building is modest in scale, but contains several elements and ideas in a flexible format. The mono-pitch tin roof of the elongated building transforms as it pushes towards the ocean, culminating in a gable end facing the sea. This part of the house contains an open-plan sitting and dining room arranged around a wood-burning stove and a large picture window framing the view of the ocean. There is a sheltered veranda to one side of the great room, while the trestle dining table is aligned with a large side window (see page 242) that frames a view of the dam and the headland beyond. The bespoke galley kitchen to the rear of the room is compact but both practical and beautifully crafted.

A long axial corridor to one side of the Quarters leads to a laundry room and shower room, two double bedrooms and then, at the end of the house, a bunkroom that sleeps three or four people. The bunkroom has a lattice window with a system of adjustable louvres that introduce light, hints of the landward aspect and fresh air that helps to cross-ventilate the house.

The main source of heating is the wood-burning stove, while water is sourced and harvested on site and stored in two storage tanks. A dam holds additional water for irrigation and grey water is also treated on the property. The only connection to mains services is a line that provides locally generated hydroelectricity. The crafted interiors also make use of recycled materials, such as the timber panelling, which comes from old apple storage boxes.

'Captain Kelly placed it on the edge of a cliff so that he could see out over the ocean, while a farmer would have built closer to the main road.'

Opposite The brick chimney anchors the house at one end, offering a subtle echo of the old farmhouse nearby.

Above A wood-burning stove, surrounded by fitted bookshelves, is a focal point for the seating area, with a picture window alongside.

Right The bunkroom at the end of the house is one of the simplest spaces, but still has a crafted, organic warmth.

Waterside and Coast

Right Openings in the tin wall bring light into the spine corridor that connects the bedrooms at one end with the living spaces at the other.

Below The new cabin sits alongside the period farmhouse overlooking the coast.

Opposite A picture window beside the fireplace in the main living area frames a key view of the coast, with a gentle inlet.

Off-Grid
Guide

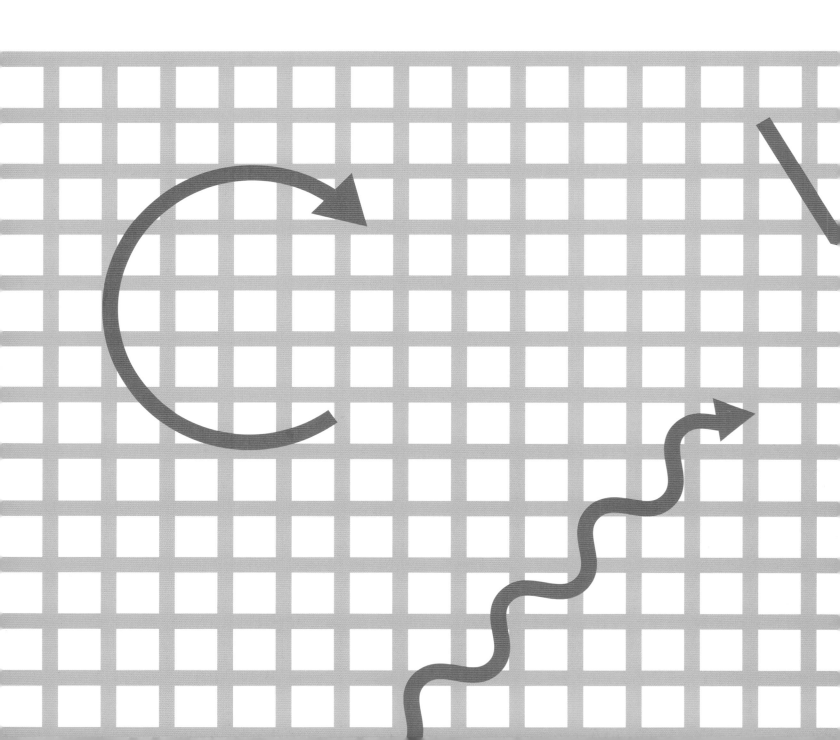

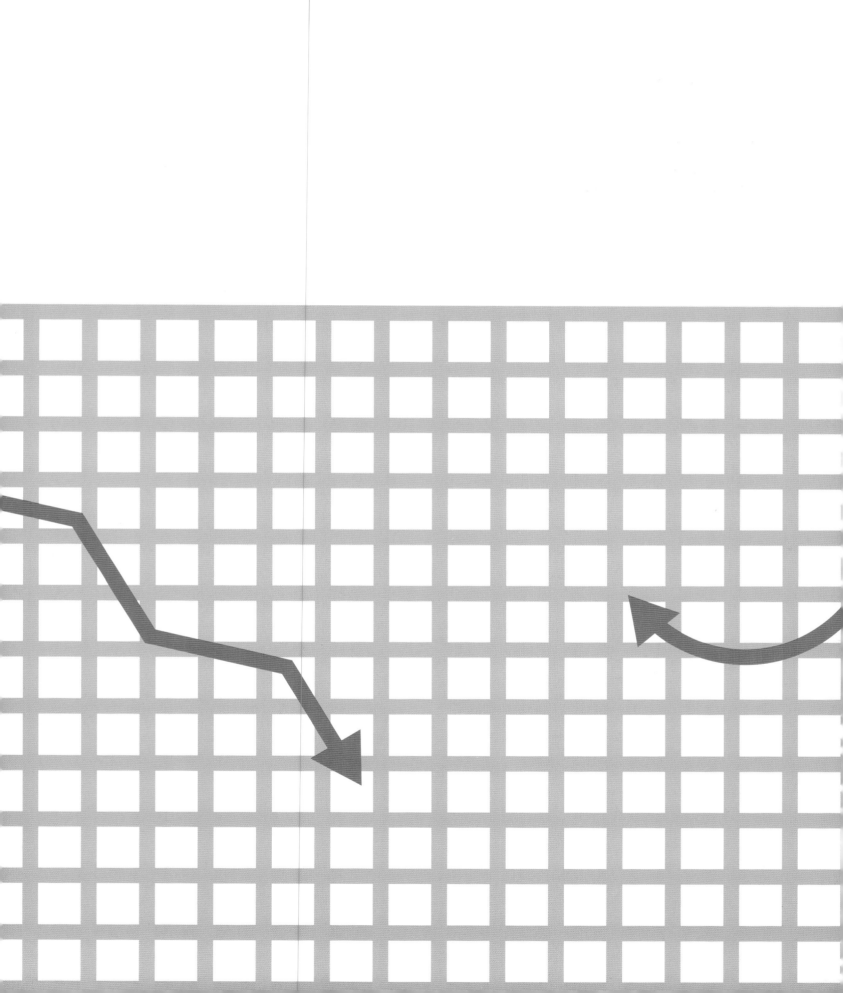

1
–
Simple Structures

Contextual design

→ The design of any bespoke home should begin with a detailed survey of the site and its specific conditions. This is especially true of an off-grid home in a remote or difficult location.

→ This should include an understanding of the landscape and its topography, in terms not only of the position of the new house but also of establishing connections with key sight lines and views.

→ Careful consideration must also be given to weather patterns, particularly any potential for extreme conditions. This includes an assessment of solar gain (see Passive Design, page 252) as well as, among other things, heavy snowfall, driving rain, strong winds and, for coastal locations, salt spray.

→ Ensure that you work with an empathetic and imaginative architect or designer who is willing to produce a contextual and site-specific response, based on a full understanding of the setting.

→ Take time to convey clearly to your architect the outcome you want, in terms both of aesthetics and of programme. A written brief helps to avoid misunderstandings.

→ Be willing to draw on the expertise and knowledge of other consultants and specialists. These should include surveyors and environmental consultants, who will be able to draw up impact assessments for the site.

→ Put time aside to keep an eye on the evolution of the project, even if you have a trusted architect and project manager in place. Involvement will help you avoid mistakes and compromises.

Planning

→ Establish legal clarity over your right to build on the plot. If in doubt, double- and triple-check the status of the site with the local planning authorities.

→ Most rural, coastal and isolated sites, particularly in national parks or other environmentally sensitive areas, come with planning restrictions that may affect how and what you can build. It is crucial that you understand and respect these restrictions.

→ Planning restrictions commonly include limits on height, size, materials and infrastructure, as well as (in coastal areas) distance from the shore. Such restrictions generally exist for good reason, and so should be seen as spurs to creativity rather than inconveniences. Engage with the local planning authorities and your architect to get a fuller picture of what may or may not be permitted on the site.

→ From the outset, consider carefully the accessibility of the site, looking at how isolation or limited infrastructure could affect the logistics of the construction process in terms of both practicality and cost.

→ Assuming that traditional utility services are either non-existent or limited, consider how water, heat and electricity can be reliably obtained (see later sections) and take advice accordingly.

→ Before any work begins on site, ensure that full and written planning permission is in place and that the local planning authorities are aware that construction is about to begin.

Programme

→ Draw up a brief or wish list for the design of the house with care and consideration, keeping in mind the impact the building might have on its site and setting.

→ Consider reducing this brief to its essentials, especially if the house is a holiday home or part-time residence that may not require the space and facilities of an everyday home.

→ Remember that a smaller floor plan means less visual and environmental impact, while also reducing the overall carbon footprint of the house, both in terms of the energy and materials required to build it and of the energy needed for heat and lighting. Essentially, a smaller house should require fewer resources of all kinds.

→ Flexible, adaptable and malleable rooms may allow a number of activities to take place in one space, such as cooking, eating and relaxing, while reducing the overall size of the structure.

→ Indoor-outdoor spaces such as verandas, porches, terraces and decks can be enticing areas for open-air living and help to reduce the physical footprint of the building. They are also essential in forging a strong connection with the surroundings.

2
–
Light Touches

Treading lightly

→ Consider the height and outline of the building within the landscape, with the aim of balancing discreetness with a strong connection to the great outdoors.

→ Work with the shape of the land, seeking to place the structure within it. Tucking a building into a hillside or among the twists and folds of the landscape shows far greater respect than imposing an alien object on the countryside or coastline.

→ Keep an open mind to vernacular influences and local architectural traditions, materials and cladding, even within a decidedly contemporary design. Such inspiration can add depth and character, as well as helping the house to sit more naturally in the region.

→ Respect the privacy of any neighbouring houses, as well as your own, in the orientation of the building and the placing of windows and terraces. Look at subtle ways of mitigating any intrusion or overlooking, while keeping in mind public rights of access to the site.

→ A compound structure, consisting of a number of smaller buildings connected by outdoor rooms, may be a more contextual solution than one larger residence, and may create more opportunities for discreet positioning within the topography.

→ Seek to keep any outbuildings or complementary structures, including garaging and equipment stores, low-slung and discreet, and in keeping with the architecture of the main house.

Preserving habitats

→ Respect existing trees, flora and fauna as far as possible. Preserving and conserving the natural planting is not only environmentally responsible but also offers the possibility of a house that is in synergy with its natural surroundings.

→ Mature trees and planting will soften the impact of the building in the landscape, while also providing shade; natural water features, such as ponds and pools, may help to cool the house in the warmer months.

→ Green roofs and other sympathetic planting around the house can play a part in offsetting the impact of a new building, as long as the plants are suited to the location and climate.

→ Raising a building on slim pillars or piloti has become a common way of lessening its impact on the land, causing minimal disturbance in comparison with embedded foundations. Raising the living space on such a supporting platform also allows the possibility of removing or updating the structure later, leaving little if any trace on the site.

→ Carefully consider and plan any groundworks that may be required, such as underground rainwater storage tanks or drilling for a ground-source heat pump. Such tasks must be undertaken in a way that causes the least damage to the site, and they may need to be offset by land conservation measures or replacement planting.

→ Avoid unnecessary disturbance to the land wherever possible. Off-grid solutions should avoid the need to install long runs of cabling, water pipes or drainage to mains sewers.

Light Houses

→ A wealth of natural sunlight in the home not only increases the quality of the spaces but also reduces the need for artificial lighting; banks of well-positioned glazing also reinforce the connection between indoors and out.

→ Most houses in the northern hemisphere face south to make the most of the sunlight, while houses in the southern hemisphere are orientated to the north. Yet the orientation must be balanced with the demands of the setting and the response to the strongest views of landscape or coast.

→ Tucking courtyards, terraces and decks into the outline of the house may help to push natural light deeper into the building, serving as light wells as much as sheltered outdoor spaces.

→ Consider maximizing light in the more 'public' parts of the house that are most commonly used in the daytime; private zones and evening spaces such as bedrooms and bathrooms generally require less natural light.

→ Open-plan layouts and light-coloured surfaces help natural light to circulate through the home; staircases can also serve as light wells when top-lit by skylights.

→ Directing light from several openings, whether windows or skylights, enhances its overall quality considerably.

→ Additional sources of light, such as solar tubes, sun pipes or sun scoops, can introduce natural light into darker corners.

3
–
Materials

Localism

→ Use locally available materials wherever possible in the interests of reducing transportation miles (which contribute to the carbon footprint of construction) and increasing contextuality.

→ Select materials that are appropriate to the climate and setting, while keeping aesthetics and sustainability in mind. Extreme settings, such as coasts or high altitudes, will demand materials that can cope with seasonal weather variation, high winds and – close to the shore – the corrosive effect of salt spray.

→ Consider the impact of weathering and seasonal extremes. Low-maintenance materials may be the best choice for holiday homes and buildings that are closed for periods when the house is not in use.

→ Balance the desire for low-maintenance materials with careful checks on any treatments applied to them, which may introduce toxicity or inappropriate chemicals to the environment.

→ Employ local skilled labour wherever possible, so as to reduce daily commuting time to the site and to draw on expertise in the unique conditions and qualities of the surroundings.

Organic Design

→ Seek sustainable sources wherever possible, including timber from responsibly managed forestry. Exercise particular caution with unaccredited suppliers. Buy timber locally or regionally, to be certain of the green benefits of sustainably grown wood.

→ Check the suitability of the timber for its intended purpose. Cladding, in particular, requires wood that is suited to the climate and conditions.

→ Make the most of the versatility and organic malleability of timber. Wood can, of course, be used in a huge variety of ways both internally and externally.

→ Common choices for timber cladding or shingles include red cedar, larch and Douglas fir, but also consider other locally or regionally grown woods.

→ Weathering often affects the colour and patina of timber, generally resulting in a natural greying.

→ Consider using recycled timber and other reclaimed materials, such as stone, brick and steel. Recycling may open up opportunities to use certain materials, such as endangered hardwoods, that would otherwise no longer be available.

→ Local and recycled stone has an 'organic' quality in design terms, and may offer a contextual solution that ties in with the local vernacular.

→ Stone has a far higher thermal mass than timber, which will require considerable insulation. On the other hand, stone, being a heavy material, is more difficult and costly to transport, and may be less suitable for structures that are raised on piloti.

→ A green roof can soften the impact of a building on the landscape, as well as adding to local biodiversity and helping to reduce the risk of flooding.

→ Remain open to other organic and traditional methods of construction, including rammed earth (or adobe/pisé), which are being revisited and reinterpreted by contemporary architects and designers.

Prefabrication

→ Prefabricating a building (or significant elements of it) in a factory greatly reduces the amount of time and labour spent constructing it on the site. This usually has positive implications in terms of cost and the carbon footprint of the project, since far less energy is spent on the daily commute to the site.

→ Accessibility is important when delivering a prefabricated or modular building to a remote site. Modules may require transportation by truck, boat or even helicopter, so size and weight are both crucial considerations.

→ Despite the embedded production energy of steel, it can be a more benign material in terms of its green credentials when it is used as part of a lightweight prefabricated building system, given the many benefits of modular construction overall.

→ Recycled materials can also play an important part in prefabricated systems, adding to the environmental benefits.

→ High levels of insulation can and should be integrated into both prefabricated modules and non-prefabricated buildings, helping to reduce heat loss and regulate the temperature of the home. Factory-made prefabricated structures generally come with higher standards of insulation.

→ Prefabrication techniques can also be used to create component parts, such as structural insulated panels (SIPs), that speed up construction while using sustainable materials and delivering high-spec insulation.

4
–
Passive Design

Insulation

→ Full and efficient insulation will conserve energy and regulate the temperature of the home, serving an essential role in any building.

→ For off-grid houses and cabins, where the availability of self-generated heat and energy may be limited, insulation becomes more vital than ever, particularly in the colder months.

→ Ensure that each part of the house is fully insulated, including the walls and the roof, and also the floor if the house is raised above the ground in any respect.

→ Remember that insulation helps to regulate the temperature of a building in both the winter and the summer, so even summerhouses should be well insulated where possible, for year-round protection from extreme variations in temperature and humidity.

→ Consider natural, organic insulating materials such as wool or hemp, as well as recycled materials, including repurposed textiles.

→ Passivhaus energy efficiency standards of construction require particularly high levels of insulation, glazing and airtightness throughout to create a carefully controlled internal environment.

→ Ensure that both architect and builders are fully aware of the implications of thermal bridging (or 'cold bridges'), which can be created when high-conductivity materials compromise, interrupt or 'bridge' the layers of insulation that envelop the building. Bridging undermines temperature control and encourages higher humidity and condensation.

Glazing

→ Windows and glazed doors are another key element of the building envelope, making a great difference to the way heat and energy are conserved or lost.

→ In colder climates, high-specification triple glazing is now being commonly used instead of double glazing.

→ Attention should also be given to the space between the layers of glazing (the overall depth of the glass unit); wider spacing generally means a higher performance.

→ Passivhaus standards generally require triple glazing, with air- or argon gas-filled units.

→ Sealed glazing units filled with argon or krypton gas will generally perform better than air-filled ones, since the gas has a lower thermal conductivity than air. Argon, which is non-toxic, reduces condensation and may help to block ultraviolet rays.

→ Even in well-sealed units, these inert gases will gradually escape over time. Triple-glazed units should still function well even after the gas is depleted, whereas double-glazed units are susceptible to fogging.

→ The frames of windows and glass doors must be as robust and well fitted as the glass itself, otherwise the benefits of such glazing can be lost. Air gaps around frames are a common cause of heat loss.

→ Also consider the impact of glazing and solar gain in the summer, looking at the provision of overhanging eaves, louvres or screens that may reduce solar gain when the sun is at its height (see Ventilation, page 254).

Heat recovery

→ Any well-designed, well-built and well-insulated new home will benefit from a mechanical ventilation with heat-recovery system (MVHR). Such systems not only help to retain heat but also circulate fresh air and reduce moisture inside the home.

→ For heavily insulated, airtight Passivhaus homes, MVHR systems are particularly important in ensuring air quality and controlling humidity.

→ Generally, MVHR systems vent stale air and replace it with fresh, filtered air from outdoors. In doing so, they capture heat and transfer it to the fresh intake, ensuring that warm air rather than cold is sent back into the building and no heat is lost to the outside.

→ MVHR systems should not be confused with air-source heat pumps, which amplify the heat taken from outside air using an electric pump.

→ Also consider the advantages of embedded heat, as could be seen in – for instance – the way that brick or stone fire surrounds hold and circulate a modest level of heat from a wood-burning stove. In a well-insulated home, this may have tangible benefits.

5
–
Solar Energy

Solar gain

→ Drawing on the natural warmth offered by the sun, or solar gain, is a simple, common-sense passive design strategy that should be explored fully.

→ In the colder months, drawing in the sun's heat through expanses of glazing will warm the house, as long as the home is well insulated and the glazing is also of a high enough standard to conserve the heat.

→ In the northern hemisphere, maximum solar gain typically comes from south-facing windows and glazing. In the southern hemisphere, the optimum direction is north.

→ Expanses of glazing also help to illuminate the home, reducing the need for artificial lighting.

→ The position of windows in the building for solar gain must be balanced or synchronized with other factors, such as privacy, maximizing important views and achieving a sense of connection between indoors and outdoors.

→ In high summer, solar gain can cause a building to overheat if care is not taken. Features that mitigate this include overhanging eaves and verandas, which reduce the effect of the high summer sun, along with flexible louvres, shutters and screens.

Photovoltaics

→ Photovoltaic panels (PVs) have become one of the most common and popular forms of renewable energy, especially for residential micropower generation.

→ PVs produce electricity as sunlight passes through solar cells made up of layers of semi-conductive material, such as silicon.

→ Before committing to PVs, consider using a power predictor kit, which should give an indication of the potential benefits of solar versus other forms of renewable energy.

→ Take advice from an energy consultant on the best position for your PV panels, as well as the number that will be required to provide adequate power for your home.

→ PVs are generally mounted on the roof of a house or outbuilding, such as a garage or barn.

→ Other options are available, including solar arrays mounted independently of a house, often in a higher position to take best advantage of the sun's movement. Ensure that you check any planning constraints before installing them, and make sure all required permissions and permits are in place.

→ As well as standard PV panels, a number of PV variants are now available, including designs that look like roof tiles.

→ You will also need an inverter unit to transform the power generated by your PV panels into electricity for use in the home.

→ Install low-energy appliances and low-energy lighting, such as LEDs, to reduce the overall electricity the house requires.

Solar thermal

→ Solar thermal panels produce hot water rather than electricity; they are sometimes used in combination with PVs.

→ Like PVs, solar thermal panels – also known as collectors – are usually mounted on roofs or outbuildings.

→ Most solar thermal panels consist of a series of tubes or flat plate collectors, and are filled with water, brine or antifreeze solutions. The liquid in the tubes heats up in the sun and is then used to heat water for home use via a heat-exchange system; the hot water is then held in storage tanks ready for use.

→ Solar thermal systems are commonly used in conjunction with other water-heating systems, which kick in when the sun is not strong enough to supply for the needs of the home. Such complementary systems include biomass boilers and electric boilers.

→ Solar thermal collectors can also be used to provide hot water for underfloor heating or radiators, depending on the number of collectors, their position and the typical strength of the sun.

6
–
Wind Power

Wind energy

→ Natural breezes and light winds can be seen as both a source of energy and a way of naturally ventilating and cooling the home at the warmest times of the year (see Ventilation).

→ The use and siting of a wind turbine for generating electricity require study of the prevailing wind speeds and careful assessment. Planning consent may also be required.

→ Wind turbines are suitable only for some locations, usually more exposed rural or coastal areas where the wind is strong enough to guarantee a return on the investment.

→ Suitable locations are not only those that are elevated. A lower setting can be appropriate for wind turbines, as long as the site is open enough or the wind is channelled in a suitable fashion.

→ Some exposed or high-altitude locations are not suitable for wind turbines, and carry the risk of significant damage in storm conditions.

→ A small wind turbine pinned to the roof of a building is seldom able to generate significant power; most domestic turbines require mounting on stand-alone masts relatively close to the home.

→ It is important to take into account the impact of masts and turbines on the local area. Masts may require foundations, and their visual impact can be a concern in sensitive locations. Turbines also produce noise, although this is relatively modest if the turbine is small.

Wind and water

→ Windmills have been used for centuries to pump water for drainage or irrigation, as well as domestic use.

→ Small-blade windmills are still in common use in Australasia, Africa, the Americas and elsewhere to pump water from wells and aquifers.

→ Most windmill water pumps work in combination with a gearbox and crankshaft, which convert the motion – or energy – created by the turning blades into a pumping motion that makes a rod pull water upwards via a piston pump.

Ventilation

→ One of the readily available benefits of wind is natural ventilation, allowing the off-grid homeowner to avoid expending energy on air-conditioning.

→ Natural cross-ventilation from open windows and doors can cool a house considerably in the warmer months, as long as circulation currents are established; Passivhaus designs also employ natural cooling from open windows in the summer.

→ Breezeways are another way of introducing cool air, with spaces that open up front to back or from side to side to allow wind to pass right through a building.

→ Such breezeways build on traditional thinking, as seen in the 'dogtrot' homes of the Midwest of America, where an open space at the heart of the house – forming an open-sided veranda under the shelter of the pitched roof – offers a cooling through current at the heart of the structure, with enclosed rooms to either side.

→ Ventilation stacks are another means of natural cooling, drawing cool air from ground level and venting hot air from the upper levels of a building. Stairwells often double as ventilation stacks, drawing the warm air upwards and expelling – or 'exhausting' – it through open skylights or vents positioned directly above.

→ Flexible louvres over ventilation gaps, often positioned alongside sealed windows, offer an easy way of drawing cool air in and through a building on warmer days. They can be fully closed and efficiently sealed in the colder months.

→ Natural ventilation will also reduce humidity. The same is true of mechanical heat-recovery ventilation (MVHR) systems (see page 253), which are commonly used in Passivhaus designs.

→ Water features near the home – such as pools and ponds – can freshen and cool it in the warmest and driest periods of the year, as well as freshening the air around outdoor rooms and terraces.

7
–
Biomass

Wood-burning stoves

→ The simplest way of generating heat from biomass is a wood-burning stove, or log-burner.

→ As long as the wood comes from sustainable sources and responsible providers, which should be local, wood-burning stoves are one of the greenest forms of renewable energy.

→ Responsible sources mean timber from sustainable forestry or wood generated as a by-product of tree surgery, agriculture, manufacturing and so on. Active replacement planting as part of sustainable forestry programmes has many ecological and environmental benefits, meaning that timber can be regarded as a carbon-neutral fuel.

→ Most of the heat from an open fire escapes through the chimney, even if a damper or draught-excluder has been fitted, although some warmth may be retained by having a brick or stone fire surround. Wood-burning stoves are much more efficient (about 75 per cent efficient rather than roughly 25 per cent for an open fire).

→ Most wood-burners are made of cast iron or steel, and the metals heat up and radiate warmth at different rates. Steel stoves warm up more quickly than cast iron, but cast iron stoves tend to retain residual heat for longer than steel wood-burners.

→ As with any form of combustion heat source or boiler, make sure the wood-burner has an efficient flue and ventilation system. Badly fitted or leaking stoves can cause carbon-monoxide poisoning, so it is also essential to fit (and regularly test) a carbon-monoxide alarm.

→ Make sure that young children are not able to touch the hot surface or flues of a wood-burning stove.

→ An off-grid home in particular might need more than one wood-burner, to heat different parts of the house.

→ Consider the position of the stove with care, looking at how it can best radiate heat through the space. Simple convection fans placed on top of a stove can push warm air through larger rooms.

→ Always burn seasoned wood, and consider the dry storage space needed to maintain a ready supply. Generally speaking, wood should be dried for one or two years; it may burn too quickly if it is left to dry for longer.

→ Multi-fuel stoves also burn other fuels, such as smokeless coal, which is not classed as carbon neutral or a renewable source of energy.

Biomass boilers

→ Biomass boilers are a green alternative to traditional gas- or oil-fired boilers, producing hot water for both heating and everyday domestic use.

→ The boilers burn wood pellets or woodchip. Compacted wood pellets, in particular, are regarded as a more efficient fuel than logs, while requiring less storage space and producing less ash.

→ The pellets or woodchip can be fed into the boiler manually or automatically from storage hoppers; sufficient storage space close to the boiler will be required.

→ Most biomass boilers have electrical controls and ignition, so electrical power is also required.

→ Waste ash must be removed regularly, weekly for most systems. The boilers also require periodic servicing.

→ Wood pellets or chips should be obtained locally where possible; they can represent an efficient and sustainable use of agricultural by-products or manufacturing waste.

Local biomass

→ Some communities are investing in mid-scale biomass plants that serve a number of houses and buildings, or an entire village. They supply hot water to each house via underground pipes.

→ Such systems can be cost-efficient and common-sense solutions. In Austria, for example, a number of villages run biomass plants using offcuts and waste from local forestry and timber production.

→ Sustainable communal solutions of this kind may not be technically off-grid, but they do provide green energy and are generally regarded as both reliable and efficient. As such, they offer tempting sources of energy for green homes.

8
–
Geothermal and Hydro

Heat pumps

→ Ground-source heat pumps draw on the natural warmth of the soil to heat the home.

→ A closed system of looped pipework is buried in the soil, either in trenches or sunk into a borehole. The borehole option should cause less disruption on sensitive sites.
→ Brine is passed through the loop of pipes and warms up as it travels underground. This heat is then amplified and concentrated as it passes through the heat pump.

→ The heated water is most commonly used to feed an underfloor heating system, but could also supply radiators.

→ The resulting water temperature is usually not very high, so the heating system must be efficient and the building well insulated.

→ A geotechnical survey is required to assess the suitability of a site for a ground-source heat pump.

→ Most heat pumps have control units powered by electricity, so a source of power will also be required. This could come from PVs or other renewable sources.

→ For maximum efficiency, some heat-pump providers recommend twenty-four-hour operation.

→ In the summer it may be possible to run a ground-source system in reverse, to cool a building.

→ Water-source heat pumps are also available; they obviously rely on a readily available supply of water. Open-loop versions extract water directly from a river, stream, lake or pond and extract heat via compression. Closed-loop systems operate in a similar way to ground-source heat pumps, sending a liquid refrigerant through sealed pipes laid in a lake or pond; the relative warmth of the lake is transferred to the refrigerant and amplified in the heat pump.

→ Air-source heat pumps draw heat from the outside air, which is again amplified, most commonly using an air-to-water system that heats water to feed underfloor heating or radiators.

Natural warmth

→ The natural warmth of the ground and soil can be used in other ways to protect and insulate a house.

→ A common way of taking advantage of the natural warmth of the land is to tuck a building partially into the slope of a hillside, so that the backdrop of earth forms a source of gentle heat. For example, bank barns were traditionally pushed into the hillside to help keep the livestock on the lower levels warm.

→ If you build in this way you must make sure the house is watertight, by using suitable barriers or membranes that prevent moisture from seeping in through the ground.

→ Similarly, green roofs with a soil base can insulate the home naturally, while camouflaging a building in the landscape and subtly enhancing biodiversity. Again, it is essential to use a membrane system to make sure the roof is watertight.

→ In some circumstances, micro hydro generators can be used to provide renewable energy.

→ Naturally, a reliable source of moving water such as a stream or river is needed, along with planning permission for the installation of the unit.

→ The successful generation of power requires an adequate and constant rate of water flow, as well as suitable water pressure to drive the blades of the micro turbine that produces the power.

→ Specialist surveys and feasibility studies will be required to assess the suitability of a water source for hydro power.

→ As long as conditions are suitable, advantages include not only renewable, clean energy but also constant power, which might not be the case with wind energy or, of course, PVs.

→ Given the sensitivity of water courses and the layers of local bureaucracy that protect them, micro hydro projects are often initiated at community level, with benefits spread to several homes or a whole village.

→ Larger hydro projects in Norway, Tasmania, Canada and elsewhere make a highly significant contribution to green energy provision using tried and trusted technology.

9
-
Water and Waste

Wells

→ Water provision is crucial to the planning of any off-grid home. If there is no mains supply it will be essential to find a reliable source of water, but since many homes and communities rely on their own wells or other sources this should be seen as a surmountable challenge.

→ Clean, potable water that is free of pollutants and contaminants is essential. Private wells are a common source, but you must take specialist advice on the site, the depth of the drilling required and the kind of pump needed to draw the water.

→ A permit is often required to drill a private well.

→ The depth of the well is a key consideration, and deeper wells are naturally more expensive to construct.

→ The key advantage of a well is reliability. Deep wells offer clean water without the need to worry about regular rainfall to top up cisterns and tanks.

→ Wind-powered pumps to draw water up from wells are a traditional alternative to electrically powered pumps (see Wind and water, page 254), and a common sight on farms and ranches.

Harvesting

→ Rainwater harvesting is another obvious source of water, but it relies on both storage capacity and relatively frequent rainfall. In areas with low rainfall or that are prone to drought, a private well may be more suitable.

→ Rainwater can be collected from roofs and gutters and stored in cisterns or tanks; tanks can be buried underground to keep them out of the way, and to ensure that the water is cool and secure.

→ Depending on the position of the tanks, a pump may be required to deliver water into the home.

→ As long as the harvested rainwater is stored correctly and cleanly, a simple filtration system should be enough to ensure that it is fit for drinking and cooking.

→ It may be possible to harvest water from streams or other local watercourses, but this commonly requires a permit and checks on the quality of the water.

→ Water is a renewable, natural resource, of course, but it must also be conserved. Conservation measures in the home include low- or dual-flush toilets and low-consumption showers instead of baths.

→ In some parts of the world, such as rural regions of Australia and parts of America, extra water cisterns or storage tanks may be required to help defend against wildfires.

→ If a swimming pool is an option, consider a natural pool, where reeds and other plants around the edges provide natural cleaning, oxygenation and filtering; however, the water must still be circulated by a pump.

Grey water and black water

→ Grey water is 'benign' waste water that has been used for washing dishes, showering and so on.

→ Grey water can be filtered and recycled for other uses, such as irrigation or filling toilet cisterns. This may have particular benefits in areas of low rainfall.

→ Black water is a polite term for sewage, i.e. human waste containing bacteria and contaminants and therefore unsuited to recycling.

→ In an off-grid home, a private septic treatment system will be required to deal with black water.

→ The most common septic system is a tank that separates the solid waste and allows it to sink to the bottom of the tank, while allowing water to flow out gradually through underground pipes and be filtered through soil, sand or gravel. Such tanks generally need to be emptied twice a year.

→ Aerobic systems generally clean black water waste more effectively than conventional systems and can be used on challenging sites without the soil conditions for a septic field. Properly designed and installed worm-based systems can deal with sewage waste more rapidly than other options and therefore usually require a single chamber of relatively modest scale.

→ Black-water treatment systems that pump treated water into open drainage channels or water courses commonly require permits.

10
–
Gardens and Landscapes

Naturalism

→ Off-grid homes tend to be in areas of particular environmental sensitivity, where a careful approach to planning and construction is required.

→ This includes all landscaping and planting around the house, and formal interventions of any kind should be kept to a minimum.

→ A naturalistic approach to landscaping seeks to dissolve any formal distinction between the surrounding landscape and the garden.

→ This usually limits fencing, walls and other formal boundaries in favour of open borders.

→ Disturbance to the land should be kept to a minimum throughout the construction process, including groundworks such as septic fields and water-storage tanks.

→ The topography of the land should be respected as far as possible, and buildings, tanks and so on slotted in discreetly. The same should be true of existing trees, which may be subject to preservation orders.

→ Planning conditions may also apply to the landscaping and/or fencing around the property.

Offset planting

→ In many cases, it's only realistic to expect that groundworks and construction will cause some degree of damage, including the loss of trees or shrubs. In such cases, offset planting may help to restore the balance and soften the impact of the house in the landscape.

→ Any new planting in such sensitive sites should be in keeping with the context, using indigenous trees, shrubs, plants and grasses that are suited to the local conditions and climate. Salty coastal conditions are particularly difficult, and extra care must be taken when choosing plants for houses by the sea.

→ New planting may provide shade around the house, helping to mitigate the impact of the summer sun in more exposed areas.

→ In areas of low rainfall, in particular, use drought-tolerant plants that require little irrigation.

→ Where irrigation is required – to support young plants, for instance – consider rainwater harvesting or grey-water recycling.

→ For self-sufficient homes, in particular, consider productive plants such as fruit bushes, olive trees and so on, to offer the extra benefit of food for the table.

Outdoor rooms

→ Planting around a veranda, terrace or deck can turn it into a welcoming outdoor room with tempting shade and freshness.

→ Outdoor rooms help to dissolve the boundaries between indoor and outdoor living space, reinforcing the connection with the landscape.

→ In areas of particular natural beauty, outdoor rooms are an essential requirement, allowing fuller appreciation of the surroundings.

→ For some people, such open-air spaces are more important than internal rooms, and offer places for cooking, dining and relaxing with a view.

→ Incorporating a choice of outdoor spaces into the design of the house creates different options for the changing seasons or times of day. A veranda or porch offers shade during the day in high summer, while a deck or roof terrace might be suited to the evenings.

→ Fire pits and outdoor barbecues turn such outdoor rooms into more social, multifunctional spaces.

→ Consider privacy when planning outdoor spaces, particularly in settings that are open to public access.

Architectural
Plans

Maison Barache p. 14

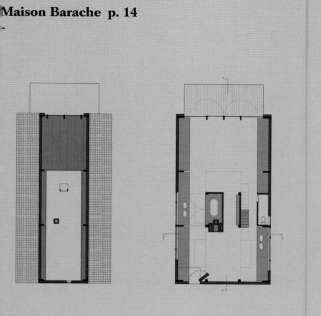

Fox Hall p. 18

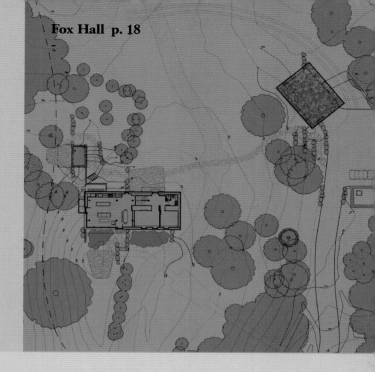

Permanent Camping p. 24

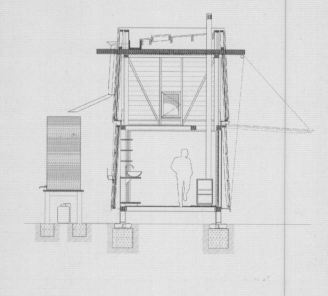

Gordon Ozarks Cabin p. 28

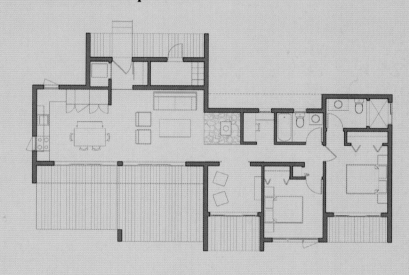

Granja Experimental Alnardo p. 34

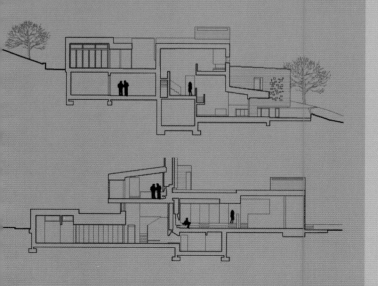

Off-Grid Retreat p. 38

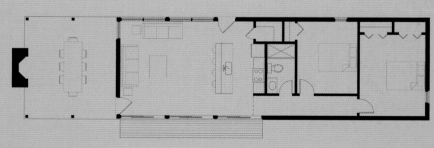

Premaydena House p. 42
-

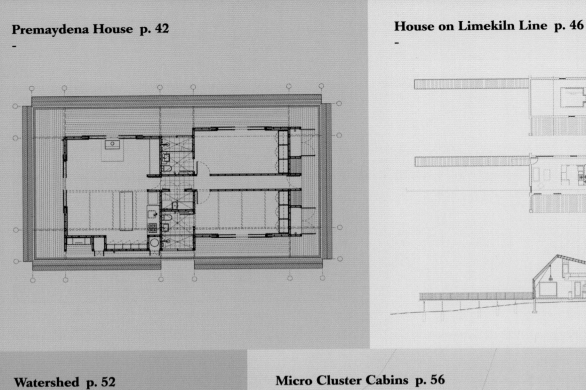

House on Limekiln Line p. 46
-

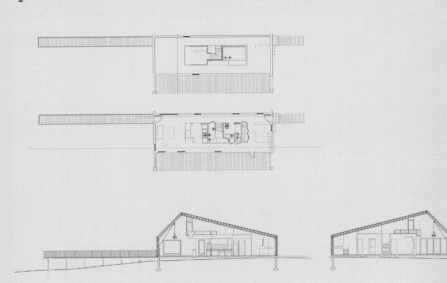

Watershed p. 52
-

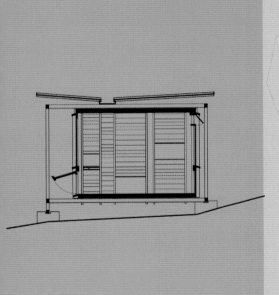

Micro Cluster Cabins p. 56
-

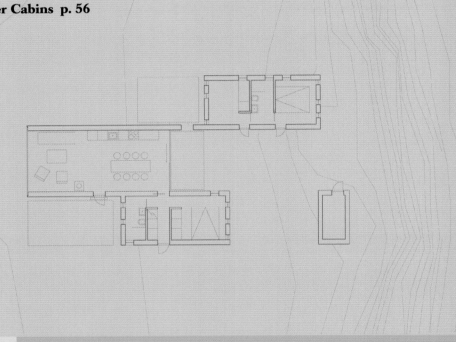

Long Island Sound House p. 62
-

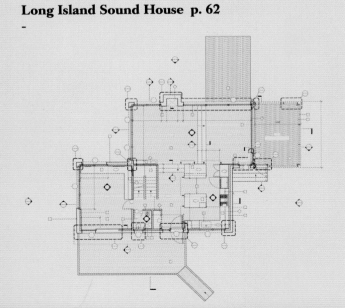

House Husarö p. 66
-

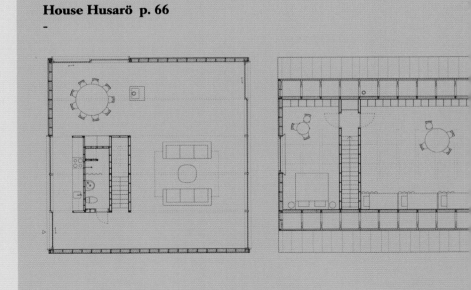

Hill Plains House p. 72
-

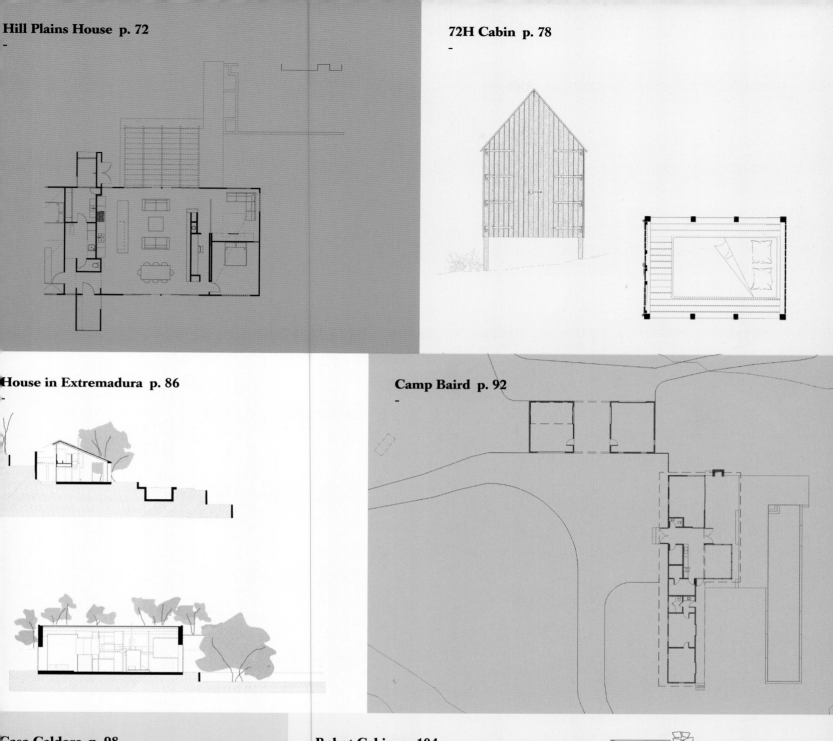

72H Cabin p. 78
-

House in Extremadura p. 86
-

Camp Baird p. 92
-

Casa Caldera p. 98
-

Rabot Cabin p. 104
-

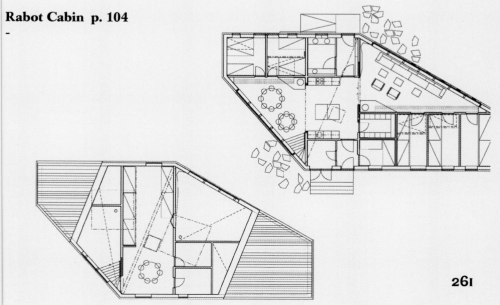

Sunshine Canyon House p. 110
-

Outside House p. 114
-

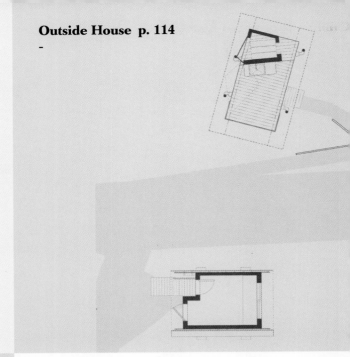

Bolton Residence p. 118
-

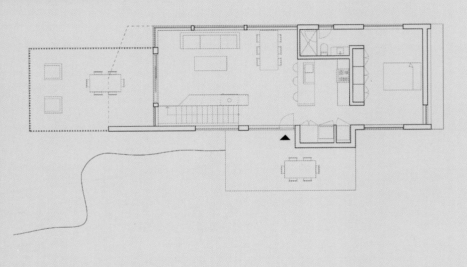

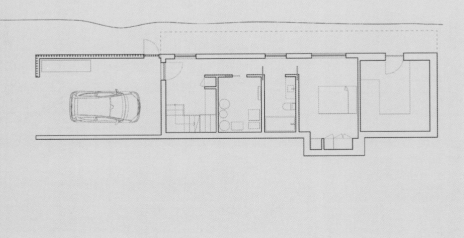

Alpine Cabin p. 130
-

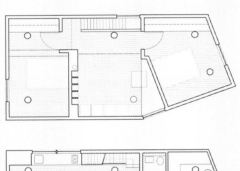

Sky House p. 124
-

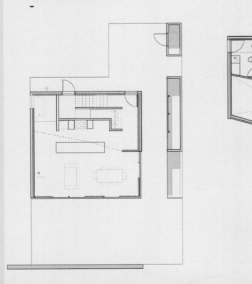

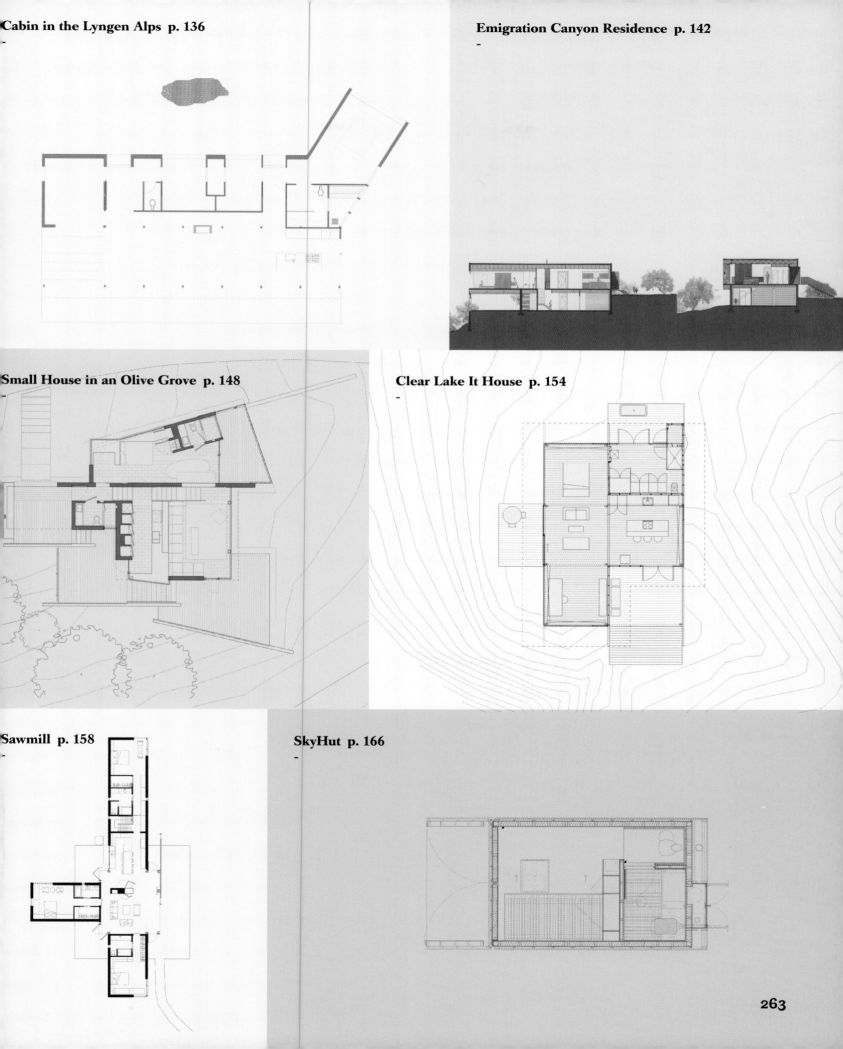

Molly's Cabin p. 174
-

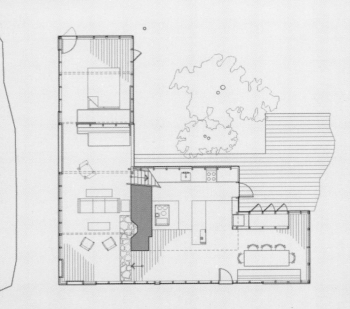

Buck's Coppice p. 178
-

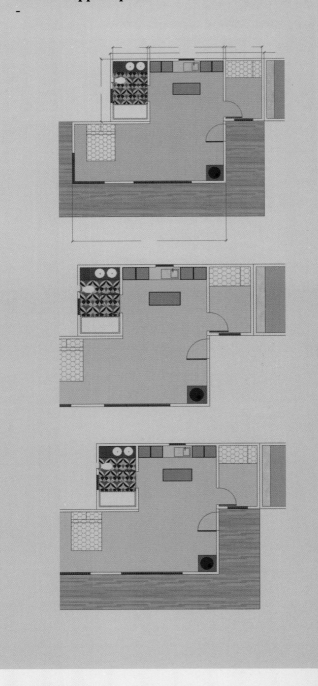

Casa Todos los Santos p. 182
-

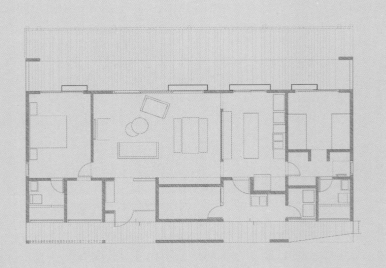

Lundnäs House p. 188
-

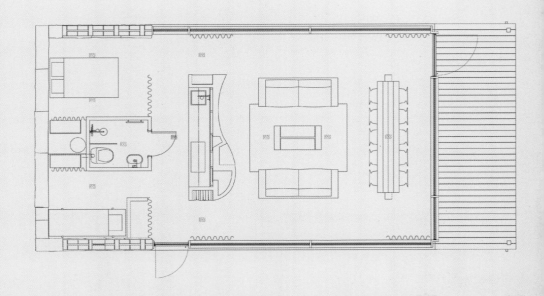

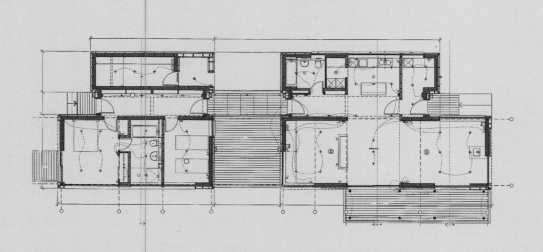

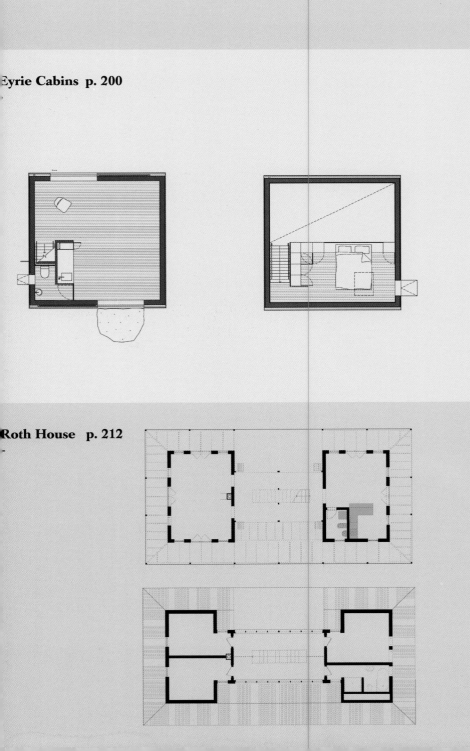

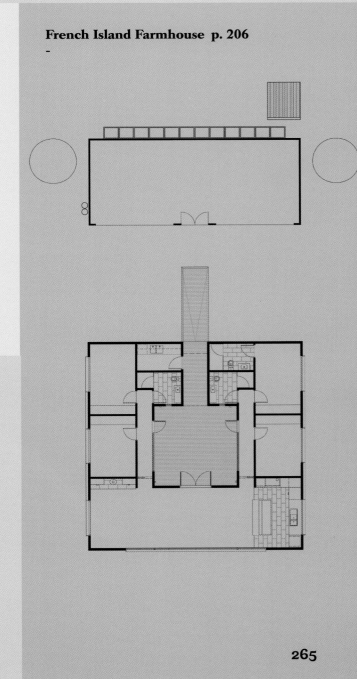

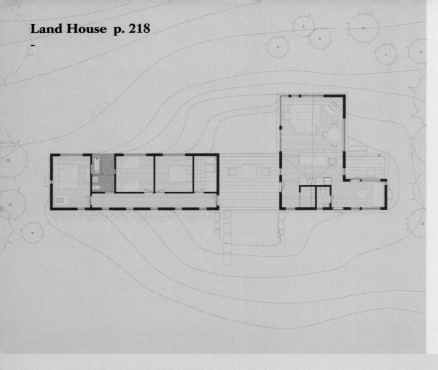

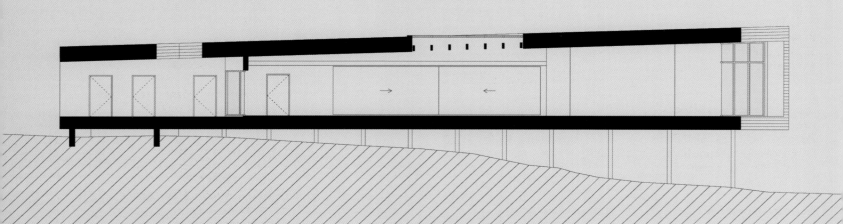

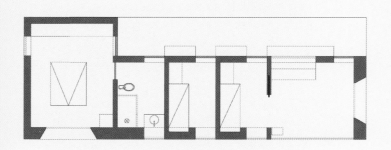

Architects and Designers

ÁBATON Arquitectura
Madrid, Spain
Principal architects: Camino Alonso,
Carlos Alonso, Ignacio Lechón
www.abaton.es

Agathom Co.
Toronto, Canada
Principal architects: Adam Thom,
Katja Aga Sachse Thom
www.agathom.com

Apio Arquitectos
Santiago, Chile
Principal architects: Carola Letelier,
Teresita Guzmán, Angie Chadwick
www.apioarquitectos.cl

arba-
Paris, France
Principal architects: Jean-Baptiste Barache,
Sihem Lamine
www.arba.pro

BarlisWedlick Architects
New York, New York, USA
Principal architects: Alan Barlis,
Dennis Wedlick, Elaine Santos (associate)
www.barliswedlick.com

Boutique Modern
Newhaven, UK
www.boutiquemodern.co.uk

Casey Brown Architecture
Sydney, Australia
Principal architects: Rob Brown,
Caroline Casey
www.caseybrown.com.au

Cheshire Architects
Auckland, New Zealand
Principal architects: Pip Cheshire,
Nat Cheshire
www.cheshirearchitects.com

Churtichaga + Quadra-Salcedo Arquitectos
Madrid, Spain
Principal architects:
Josemaria de Churtichaga,
Cayetana de la Quadra-Salcedo
www.chqs.net

Delin Arkitektkontor
Stockholm, Sweden
Principal architect: Buster Delin
www.delinarkitektkontor.se

DEN Architecture
Miami, Florida, USA
Principal architects: Germán Brun,
Lizmarie Esparza
www.den-arc.com

DUST
Tucson, Arizona, USA
Principal architects: Cade Hayes,
Jesús Robles
www.dustdb.com

FLOAT Architectural Research & Design
Eugene, Oregon, USA
Principal architect: Erin Moore
www.floatwork.com

Henning Larsen Architects
Copenhagen, Denmark
Principal architects: Mette Kynne Frandsen,
Louis Becker, Ingela Larsson
www.henninglarsen.com

Jarmund/Vigsnæs AS Arkitekter MNAL
Oslo, Norway
Principal architects: Einar Jarmund,
Håkon Vignæs
www.jva.no

Jeanarch
Sweden
Principal architect: Jeanna Berger
www.jeanarch.com

John Wardle Architects
Melbourne, Australia
Principal architect: John Wardle
www.johnwardlearchitects.com

Lai Cheong Brown
Melbourne, Australia
Principal architects: Rowan Brown,
Christina Lai Cheong
www.laicheongbrown.com

Malcolm Davis Architecture
San Francisco, California, USA
Principal architect: Malcolm Davis
www.mdarch.net

Mary Arnold-Forster
Scotland, UK
Principal architect: Mary Arnold-Forster
www.maryarnold-forster.co.uk

Midland Architecture
Pittsburgh, Pennsylvania, USA and
Columbus, Ohio, USA
Principal architects: Matt Diersen,
Greg Dutton
www.midlandarch.com

Misho + Associates
Hobart, Australia
Principal architect: Misho James Vasiljevich
www.misho.com.au

Modersohn & Freiesleben
Berlin, Germany
Principal architects: Johannes Modersohn,
Antje Freiesleben
www.mofrei.de

Architects and Designers

_naturehumaine
Montreal, Canada
Principal architect: Stéphane Rasselet,
www.naturehumaine.com

Olson Kundig
Seattle, Washington State, USA
Principal architects: Jim Olson, Tom Kundig
www.olsonkundig.com

Omas: Works
Toronto, Ontario, Canada and
New York, New York, USA
Principal architects: Brian O'Brian,
Carl Muehleisen
www.omasworks.com

Oopeaa
Helsinki, Finland
Principal architect: Anssi Lassila
www.oopeaa.com

Petra Gipp Arckitektur
Stockholm, Sweden
Principal architect: Petra Gipp
www.gipparkitektur.se

PLATFORM Architecture + Design
Victoria, Canada
Principal architect: Jesse Garlick
www.p4ma.com

Reiulf Ramstad Arkitekter
Oslo, Norway
Principal architects: Reiulf Ramstad,
Kristin Stokke Ramstad
www.reiulframstadarchitects.com

Renée del Gaudio Architecture
Boulder, Colorado, USA
Principal architect: Renée del Gaudio
www.rdg-architecture.com

Room II
Hobart, Australia
Principal architects: Aaron Roberts,
Thomas Bailey
www.room11.com.au

Ryall Sheridan Architects
New York, New York, USA
Principal architects: Bill Ryall, Ted Sheridan
www.ryallsheridan.com

Saunders Architecture
Bergen, Norway
Principal architect: Todd Saunders
www.saunders.no

Scott & Scott Architects
Vancouver, Canada
Principal architects: David Scott, Susan Scott
www.scottandscott.ca

Sparano + Mooney Architecture
Los Angeles, California, USA and
Salt Lake City, Utah, USA
Principal architects: John Sparano,
Anne Mooney
www.sparanomooney.com

Stinessen Arkitektur
Tromsø, Norway
Principal architect: Snorre Stinessen
www.snorrestinessen.com

Studio Joseph
New York, New York, USA
Principal architect: Wendy Evans Joseph
www.studiojoseph.com

Studio Moffitt
Edinburgh, UK
Principal architect: Lisa Moffitt
www.studiomoffitt.com

Taalman Architecture
Los Angeles, California, USA
Principal architect: Linda Taalman
www.taalmanarchitecture.com +
www.tkithouse.com

Tham & Videgård Arkitekter
Stockholm, Sweden
Principal architects: Bolle Tham,
Martin Videgård
www.thamvidegard.se

**Waind Gohil +
Potter Architects**
London, UK
Principal architects: Phil Waind,
James Potter, Sonya Gohil
www.wgpa.co.uk

Wolveridge Architects
Melbourne, Australia
Principal architect: Jerry Wolveridge
www.wolveridge.com.au

Author Biography

Dominic Bradbury is a writer and journalist specializing in architecture and design. His many books include *Mid-Century Modern Complete, Modernist Design Complete, The Iconic House* and *The Iconic Interior*, all published by Thames & Hudson. He contributes to many newspapers and magazines internationally, including *The Financial Times, The Times, The Telegraph, Wallpaper** and *House & Garden*. He lives in Norfolk, England, and is also a design consultant and visiting lecturer.

Author Acknowledgments

The author would like to express his sincere gratitude to all of the architects, designers and home owners featured in this book for their much valued assistance and support. Thanks are also due to graphic designer Therese Vandling, and Lucas Dietrich, Fleur Jones and Evie Tarr at Thames & Hudson, as well as Gordon Wise, Niall Harmann, Richard Powers, Carrie Kania and Faith Bradbury.

Picture Credits

Photography

4: Joe Fletcher; **14–17:** Celine Clanet; **18–23:** Richard Powers; **24–27:** Penny Clay; **28–33:** Greg Clark; **34–37:** Hufton + Crow; **38–40:** Jay Guillion; **41:** Laura Petrilla; **42–45:** Peter Whyte; **46–51:** Shai Gil; **52–55:** J. Gary Tarleton; **56–61:** Reiulf Ramstad Arkitekter; **62–65:** Ty Cole; **66–71:** Åke E:son Lindman; **72–77:** Richard Powers; **78–81:** Jeanna Berger; **86–91:** Belen Imaz; **92–97:** Joe Fletcher; **98–103:** Esto/Jeff Goldberg; **104L:** Jan Inge Larsen; **104–105:** Tommy Eliassen; **106:** Einar Aslaksen; **107T:** Svein Arne Brygfjeld; **107B–109:** Jan Inge Larsen; **110–13:** David Lauer Photography; **114–17:** Olivier Koning; **118–23:** Adrien Williams; **124–29:** Theo and Theresa Morrison; **130–35:** Scott & Scott Architects; **136–40, 141B(L&R):** Bent Raanes; **141TR:** Siggen Stinessen; **142:** Dustin Aksland; **143:** Dennis Mecham; **144–46L:** Dustin Aksland; **146–47:** Bryan Allen; **148–53:** Elliott Kaufman Photography; **154–65:** Richard Powers; **166–69:** Anthony Coleman; **174–77:** Paul Orenstein; **178–80:** Sandra Whipham; **182–87:** Alejandra Valenzuela; **188–93:** Patric Johansson; **194–99:** Huntley Hedworth; **200–205:** Jeremy Toth; **206–11:** Jaime Diaz-Berrio; **212–17:** Johannes Modersohn; **218–23:** Shai Gil; **224–29:** Benjamin Hosking; **230–35:** Bent René Synnevåg; **236–41:** Siggen Stinessen and Snorre Stinessen; **242–47:** Richard Powers

Architectural Plans

Credits are listed clockwise from top left on each page.

259: Jean-Baptiste Barache; BarlisWedlick Architects; DEN Architecture; Midland Architecture; Henning Larsen Architects; Casey Brown Architecture; **260:** Misho + Associates; Studio Moffitt; Reiulf Ramstad Arkitekter; Tham & Videgård Arkitekter; Ryall Sheridan Architects; FLOAT Architectural Research and Design; **261:** Wolveridge Architects; JeanArch; Malcolm Davis Architecture; Jarmund Vigsnæs; DUST; ÁBATON Arquitectura; **262:** Renée del Gaudio Architecture; FLOAT Architectural Research and Design; Scott & Scott Architects; PLATFORM Architecture + Design; _Naturehumaine; **263:** Stinessen Arkitektur; Sparano + Mooney Architecture; Taalman Architecture; Waind Gohil + Potter Architects; Olson Kundig; Studio Joseph; **264:** Agathom Co.; Boutique Modern; Delin Arkitektkontor; Apio Arquitectos; **265:** Mary Arnold-Forster; Lai Cheong Brown; Modersohn & Freiesleben; Cheshire Architects; **266:** Omas:Works; Room 11; Saunders Architecture; John Wardle Architects; Stinessen Arkitektur

Index

Page numbers in *italics* refer to architectural plans

Author Dedication

To Florence

On the front cover: Cheshire Architects: Eyrie Cabins (see page 200); photographer: Jeremy Toth.

On the back cover (clockwise from top left): Studio Moffitt: House on Limekiln Line (see page 46), photographer: Shai Gil; Tham & Videgård: House Husarö (see page 66), photographer: Åke Eson Lindman; _naturehumaine: Bolton Residence (see page 118), photographer: Adrien Williams; Jarmund Vigsnæs: Rabot Cabin (see page 104), photographer: Jan Inge Larsen; Delin Arkitektkontor: Lundnäs House (see page 188), photographer: Patric Johansson; Scott & Scott Architects: Alpine Cabin (see page 130), photographer: Scott & Scott. Page 4: Malcolm Davis Architecture: Camp Baird (see page 92).

Designed by Therese Vandling

First published in 2019 in the United States of America by Thames & Hudson Inc., 500 Fifth Avenue, New York, New York 10110

www.thamesandhudsonusa.com

Library of Congress Control Number 2018946039

ISBN 978-0-500-02142-2

Printed in China by Midas Printing International Ltd